general

THE PAROCHIAL LIBRARIES
OF THE CHURCH OF ENGLAND

He that stelles this Boke he shalbe
hanked a pon on hoke Behind the
kechen dor.

BENNET NELLSON, 15th cent,
(quoted in Lincolnshire Archives Committee
Archivist's Report, no. 9, 1957–8, p. 17.)

THE PAROCHIAL LIBRARIES
OF THE
CHURCH OF ENGLAND

Report of a Committee appointed by the
CENTRAL COUNCIL FOR THE CARE OF CHURCHES
to investigate the Number and Condition
of Parochial Libraries
belonging to the Church of England

With an Historical Introduction
Notes on early Printed Books and their Care and
an Alphabetical List of Parochial Libraries
Past and Present

LONDON
Published in conjunction with the College of the Faith by
THE FAITH PRESS LTD

FIRST PUBLISHED IN 1959

© The Central Council for the Care of Churches 1959

PRINTED IN GREAT BRITAIN
in 12-pt. Baskerville type
BY THE FAITH PRESS LTD
LEIGHTON BUZZARD

FOREWORD BY
THE ARCHBISHOP OF CANTERBURY

NEARLY ten years ago I received a letter from the Secretary of the Bibliographical Society drawing attention to the neglected state of many Parochial Libraries. The letter interested me, since from time to time, both in Cheshire and elsewhere, I have had the good fortune to see parochial libraries well cared for and possessing great interest. Accordingly I wrote to the Central Council for the Care of Churches drawing their attention to this matter, and asking whether they could promote some enquiries. The Council has done far more than I ever expected. The task of making a full Report on Parochial Libraries is difficult and complicated, but undeterred by any fears the Central Council appointed a Committee which has produced the material which follows in this volume. The initiative has come from the Central Council: the success of the work is largely due to the able editorship of Mr. Neil Ker, who was a member of the Committee.

I am sure that many people will look at this volume and find it full of interest of one kind and another. The existence of these Parochial Libraries scattered up and down the country has a significance for all those who care about the social history of our country in past generations, and about the kind of intellectual and cultural outlook among the clergy of those distant days. The Report will move some of us to a degree of regret that the modern conditions of stress and strain and hustle have really made much of the scholarly thought and meditation of earlier generations beyond our reach. It is at least a reminder to us that, however difficult, the clergy of to-day, and indeed the laity too, must make it possible to keep themselves well read and well informed: and that not only in the literature which deals with the affairs of this world, but above all in the literature which reveals in one way or another the glories of God and of His manifold works for man's salvation.

It is hardly necessary to say that all concerned with these surviving libraries should be most careful to preserve and care for them along the lines proposed by the Central Council's Committee in the Recommendations which this Report contains.

GEOFFREY CANTUAR.

ACKNOWLEDGMENTS

THE Committee wish to acknowledge with grateful thanks the useful help given by a great many people in connection with the preparation of this report, especially Mr. F. C. Morgan, their indefatigable Honorary Secretary, upon whom the task of circularizing incumbents and other custodians of parochial libraries has mainly fallen, Miss M. S. G. Hands (now Mrs. Neil MacLeod) and Mr. Neil Ker, who undertook to act as Editor and to prepare the material for the press. Valuable help was given to Mr. Ker by the S.P.C.K. and the Associates of Dr. Bray, who gave access to their records, Miss Joan Petersen, Librarian to the Central Council, Miss Molly Barrett, who drew attention to the 'Notitia Parochialis' in Lambeth Palace Library, and Mr. Malcolm Parkes, who made excerpts of the entries in it relating to libraries, Miss Claire Cross, Mr. Ian Doyle, Mr. F. G. Emmison, Miss Joyce Godber, Miss Margot Johnson, Mr. Paul Kaufman, Mr. A. N. L. Munby, Mr. Graham K. Scott, who allowed use to be made of material of his own relating to the history of institutional libraries, Mr. George Smith, Mr. J. E. Vaughan, Mr. Peter Wallis, and Miss Dorothy Williamson.

The Committee would like to thank Mr. Lawrence Tanner for allowing their meetings to be held in Westminster Abbey Library, which provided a most congenial setting for their work.

Their most grateful thanks are due to the College of the Faith for giving financial help with the preparation of the text for the press and for undertaking its publication : also to the photographers who have supplied the illustrations.

Last, but not least, it is their pleasant duty to acknowledge the patient co-operation of incumbents and others who have replied to their questionnaires.

CONTENTS

B

ILLUSTRATIONS

HISTORICAL INTRODUCTION

I. LIBRARIES IN CHURCHES AND PARSONAGES
FIFTEENTH TO TWENTIETH CENTURIES

I

MANY parish churches contain a number of books which varies in different places from two or three volumes to several hundreds. It is often asked how they came to be there, and why dusty, shabby, and apparently out-of-date books should be preserved. It is the purpose of this publication to show that these books are important possessions, handed down from the past, to be valued in the same way as other treasures. They are part of the cultural heritage of which we are now the trustees. Their interest is great, for they are evidence of historical events, and give us glimpses of the way our forebears dealt with the problems of their time, as well as material for the study of political and social life.

As we would expect, these libraries were mainly theological. We find Bibles in English, Hebrew, Latin, Greek, or in two or more languages arranged in parallel columns; also commentaries on the Bible. The Fathers of the Church, such as Augustine, Chrysostom and Ambrose, are represented, and from the sixteenth century onwards, there was a continuous stream of theology including doctrine, exposition and controversy. The Roman claims naturally demanded attention, and works on both sides survive. There are collections of sermons, many of which show an unexpected wealth of imagery and force of expression. It has been said of seventeenth-century sermons that 'they are grave, dry, abstruse, dreadful; to our debilitated attentions they are hard to follow ... they are devoted to a theology that yet lingers in the memory of mankind only through certain shells of words long since emptied of their original meaning. Nevertheless, these writings are monuments of vast learning, and of a stupendous intellectual energy both in the men who produced them and in the men who listened to them. . . . They were conceived by noble minds; they are themselves noble. They are superior to our jests. We may deride them if we will; but they are not derided.' [1]

---

[1] M. C. Tyler, *A history of American literature*, vol. 1, 1607–76, 1879, pp. 192–3.

2

The keeping of books in parish churches was a common practice in the Middle Ages, as appears from wills and inventories. Probably most churches possessed some books other than service-books in the fifteenth century. There were, for example, a dozen such at S. Margaret's, New Fish Street, London, in 1476. They are listed, together with forty-seven service-books, in the churchwardens' records, and, as commonly, were chained.[2] Probably most churches had fewer books than this, but the principal churches are likely to have had more. Thus Boston church had a 'libraria' in the second half of the fifteenth century. Copies of the Poly-chronicon and Dieta Salutis and other books were bequeathed to it in 1457.[2a] A common-law book was bequeathed to it in 1469.[2b] These books were, no doubt, part of a larger collection.

Medieval manuscripts like those at Boston were already old-fashioned by the time of the Reformation. The invention of printing, not the change of religion, was primarily responsible for their disuse. But it is likely that in most places such books as there were, whether printed or manuscript, were thrown out, along with the old service-books, at or soon after the Reformation. Incumbents had no longer any use for a popular priest's guide like Pupilla Oculi, whether in print or in manuscript. A few medieval service-books and Bibles belong now to the churches to which they belonged before the Reformation, but the churches have not owned them continuously since the Reformation.[3] No church possesses any of its pre-Reformation library books, except possibly All Saints, Bristol.

3

During the half century after the Reformation, the only institutional libraries in England were those which had survived from the Middle Ages, often in a rather struggling fashion, in the two universities and attached to the ancient cathedrals and to the colleges of Eton and Winchester, and those established in a few of the colleges and schools founded in the middle and second half of the century. Nothing that we should call a library is known to have existed in a parish church in this period. Reading matter for the clergy was provided, however, to some extent in the old way, by bequest, and reading matter for the laity was provided by authority. An order of 1538 required the placing of English

[2] C. Wordsworth and H. Littlehales, *The old Service-books of the English Church*, 1904, pl. II.
[2a] *Richmondshire Wills*, Surtees Soc., vol. 26 (1853), p. 2.
[2b] *Registrum Cancellaru*, vol. II, Oxford Historical Soc., vol. 94, 1932, p. 307.
[3] See pp. 108–11 for pre-Reformation service-books and Bibles in manuscript belonging to Bristol (S. Thomas the Martyr), Buckingham, London (S. Peter Cornhill), Ranworth, and Wollaton.

Bibles in churches.[4] In 1547 King Edward's injunctions required incumbents to provide the Bible 'of ye largest volume in English' and 'the Paraphrasis of Erasmus also in Englishe vpon the Gospelles, and the same sette up in some conuenient place, with in the sayed Churche, that they haue cure of, whereas their Parishioners maye moste commodiously resorte vnto the same, and read the same.'[5] These injunctions were repeated by Queen Elizabeth in 1559.[6] The repetition was necessary because what had been 'sette up' by King Edward had been taken down again by Queen Mary. The following note may not refer to books in a church, but it probably shows what happened to books in many churches between 1553 and 1558: 'Memorandum that i burnyd all the boockes. In primys a bybyll of rogers translatyon the paraphrases yn Englysche A communyon boocke Halles cronekylles the byshop of canterberyes booke Latimers sermonttes Hopers sermontes A psalter.'[7] In Elizabeth's reign and James's and later, the Bible, the Homilies of the Church, the Paraphrases and some other books, notably Foxe's *Book of Martyrs*,[8] and Jewel's *Works*,[9] were so widely distributed by injunction and otherwise, that an appreciable number have survived the wear and tear of three or four hundred years. They were, and, in a few cases still are, chained to reading desks. Lists of them have been compiled,[10] but these are necessarily far from complete, since no reliable list can be made except after a detailed survey, county by county. Very few of these 'desk libraries' have as many as a dozen books. The alphabetical list attached to this Report records a few of them, either because of their exceptional size (e.g. Ecclesfield, Sleaford, Sutton Courtenay, Wootton Wawen), or

[4] Second Royal Injunctions of Henry VIII, 1538. 'Item, that ye shall provide on this side the feast of Easter next coming, one book of the whole Bible of the largest volume in English.' See *Visitation Articles and Injunctions of the Period of the Reformation*, ed. W. H. Frere, vol. 2 (Alcuin Club Collections, vol. 15, 1910), p. 35.

[5] *Iniunccions geuen by Edward the sixte*, 1547, sign. (a. iiij verso). These are also given by Frere, *op. cit.*, p. 117.

[6] *Iniunccions geuen by the Queenes Maiestie*, 1559, sign. A. iii.

[7] A note at the end of *Autores historiæ ecclesiasticæ*, Bas., 1557, in a contemporary London binding, no. 211 of the books in the parochial library at Cartmel, Lancashire.

[8] The Canons of 1571 required that the Archbishops and Bishops, Deans, Canons, and Archdeacons should possess at home, in the hall or dining room, where they could be perused by visitors, the 'Bible of the largest volume,' (i.e. the Bishops' Bible of 1568), Foxe's *Book of Martyrs* and 'alios quosdam similes libros ad religionem appositos.' Deans were required to provide the same books in the cathedrals, but the churchwardens of parish churches were only required to provide, in addition to the Prayerbook and Book of Homilies, the 'Bible of the largest volume.' Some, no doubt, thought it wise to place a more liberal interpretation on the Canon. Thus, according to the vestry minutes of S. Michael, Cornhill, in the City of London, it was agreed on January 11, 1571–2, 'That the book of Martyrs of Mr. Foxe and the paraphrases of Erasmus shal be bought for the church and tyed with a chayne to the Egle bras.' See *Accounts of the Churchwardens of S. Michael, Cornhill, 1456–1608*, ed. W. H. Overall, 1871, p. 167.

[9] Archbishop Bancroft wished that 'every parish in England' should have a copy of Jewel's *Works* (letter of 27 July 1610 printed by E. Cardwell, *Documentary Annals* (2nd ed. 1844), II, 160).

[10] See W. Blades, *Books in Chains*, 1890, J. C. Cox and A. Harvey *English Church Furniture*, 1907, pp. 338–40 and the supplementary lists in *The Library*, vol. 3 (1891), p. 179 (Minehead, by R. G. C. Proctor), pp. 270–3, 441–5, and in *Notes and Queries*, 12th Series, vol. 12 (1923), p. 495, by Canon J. M. J. Fletcher.

because they form the nucleus of a larger library founded at a later date (e.g. Cartmel and Bridlington). Collections with six to a dozen books are at Hodnet in Shropshire, where the desk is still in use, Abingdon in Berkshire, Enstone in Oxfordshire, Melton Mowbray in Leicestershire, Winslow in Buckinghamshire, and Wrington in Somerset.[11]

4

The first establishment of libraries of some size independent of universities, cathedrals, colleges and schools, comes not surprisingly in the great period at the end of the sixteenth century, which is in Oxford especially notable for the foundation of the Bodleian Library, and the thorough reformation of the libraries at Merton College, All Souls College and S. John's College. We read of a room called the library in the church at Leicester in 1586–7 and in the church at Newcastle in 1597. At Bury St. Edmunds various donors combined to form a church library in 1595: contemporary records of the foundation are lacking, but the facts can be ascertained from inscriptions in the books themselves. At Grantham Francis Trigge founded a library in the church by will dated 20 October 1598. At Ipswich William Smart bequeathed books to the church by will dated 8 January 1598–9.

The wording of wills and other records of the use and ownership of these libraries and of other libraries founded in the next century in towns suggest that town libraries and church libraries are not easily distinguishable.[12] It is no coincidence that, except at Norwich, town libraries were not set up in towns where there were already cathedral libraries. There is no distinction, except in the placing, between Trigge's gift of a library to the Alderman and Burgesses of Grantham for the use of the clergy and others in the town and soke of Grantham and in the County of Lincoln, and Archbishop Harsnett's gift of a library in 1631 to the Bailiffs and Corporation of Colchester for the use of the clergy of the town and other divines. Trigge's was put in the church, and is usually thought of as a church library; Harsnett's was not. A convenient place for a library was all important. Henry Bury's bequest of money to buy books for the common use of the parish of Manchester in 1634 was conditional on their having 'a convenient place of their owne.' The libraries kept in buildings apart from the church, Norwich, Ipswich (after 1612), Bristol,

---

[11] A photograph of the desk at Wrington taken in July 1890 is in the Bodleian Library (shelfmark 2589.b.4): it shows eight chained books.

[12] School libraries and town libraries may also be difficult to distinguish. The library founded by Bishop Parkhurst at Guildford Grammar School in 1573 is, and was already at the end of the sixteenth century, considered to be a school library, but according to the terms of Parkhurst's will, his gift was 'to the Lybrarie of the same Town ioyning to the schole' (G. C. Williamson, *Guildford in the olden Time*, 1904, p. 105).

Colchester, and Leicester (after 1632); [13] the libraries kept in parish churches but under lay control, having been formed by the citizens or entrusted by their donors to the town governors, Barnstaple, Grantham, King's Lynn, Manchester, Marlborough, Newark, Newcastle, Totnes, Wisbech; the libraries which seem to have been in the control of the church, Bury, Oakham, Stamford, all contained the same sort of books and were formed with the same object, the advancement of learning. The books are for students, and, to a large extent, in Latin. They are, in fact, a selection of the books which would have been found at this time in a college library at Oxford or Cambridge, and may be thought of as college libraries in miniature transported to the provinces for the use mainly of the local clergy.

At the end of the seventeenth century libraries were to be found in the parish churches of a score of towns. A dozen more came into existence at the turn of the century. Of these Reigate, founded in 1701 for the use of the 'freeholders, vicar and inhabitants,' is the best documented and perhaps the most interesting.

5

Outside the towns only a very small number of libraries were founded, so far as we know, before the last two decades of the seventeenth century. The founder of one of them, Tankersley (1615), used a phrase which was much used later: the books were given to the incumbent 'and his successors for ever.' At Langley Marish (1631) the library was for the 'perpetual benefit' of the incumbent and other clergy. At King's Norton (1662?) the library was given to the parish and kept in the Grammar School in the churchyard. At Chirbury (1677) the library was 'for the Use of the Schoolmaster or any other of the Parishioners': it, too, was to be placed in the schoolhouse in the churchyard. These are all libraries in which books in Latin were numerous. In contrast to them, the libraries founded by Humphrey Chetham, d.1653, in the churches of Bolton, Gorton, Turton, and Manchester contained only books in English and were 'for the edification of the common people'—in the words of Chetham's will.

Chetham's foundations are parochial libraries in the sense which seems now the obvious sense. The term was not, however used at this time, nor at all, so far as can be discovered, until the last years of the seventeenth century, when it was applied to the type of library then in

[13] For the history of the Norwich, Bristol, and Colchester libraries, see G. A. Stephen, *Three Centuries of a City Library*, 1917; N. Mathews, *Early Printed Books and Manuscripts in the City Reference Library, Bristol*, 1899; G. Goodwin, *Catalogue of the Harsnett Library at Colchester*, 1888.

17

C

favour, that reserved for the exclusive use of the incumbent and his successors.

6

A crisis in the history of libraries in churches occurred about 1680. Before this time only a few libraries had been founded and most of these were in towns. During the next half-century, however, many libraries were founded and mainly in those churches where the incumbents were least likely to have books of their own. The idea of placing libraries deliberately in the poorer livings throughout the country occurred, it seems, to Sir Roger Twysden (d. 1672).[14] It was put into practice in a small way by Barnabas Oley in 1685 and later by a committee of the Society for Promoting Christian Knowledge. Its best known and most enthusiastic advocate was Thomas Bray (1656–1730), whose writings encouraged many people to found libraries. The provision of a parochial library became a proper object of charity. 'Have you a Parochial Library?' was a question asked at episcopal and archidiaconal visitations.[15] Some of the country clergy left books to their successors for ever, and some of the nobility and gentry founded libraries in their local churches, for example at Astley, Bassingbourne, Bromham, and More. The number of libraries thus founded in country churches and parsonages 'to be an agreable Companion to a Man of Letters destitute of Books in a solitary Country'[16] was no doubt much larger than would appear from the alphabetical list attached to the Report. Many unrecorded 'standing' libraries are likely to exist in parsonages and many, once there, are likely to have perished from the ordinary causes or because they were dispersed with the goods of deceased incumbents (cf. Flaxley, Sible Hedingham, Tideford). Many of the existing libraries are of particular interest, because they introduce us to the books of the individual donors, usually a mixture of Latin and English, including pamphlets and schoolbooks. Inscriptions often show that books were bought during their owner's tenure of a college fellowship at Oxford or Cambridge. Thus we have the books of John Okes of S. Edmund Hall in the Wotton-under-Edge collection, the books of Cavendish Nevile of University College in the Norton collection, and the books of William Beasley of King's College, in the Mentmore collection.

7

In 1685 Barnabas Oley, fellow of Clare College, Cambridge, prebendary of Worcester and vicar of Great Gransden, required his executor to give

[14] T. Bray, *Bibliotheca Parochialis*, 1697, sign. a.3. verso.
[15] For example in 1716 (Canterbury, Norwich), 1722 (Oxford), 1735 (Bristol), 1759 (Oxford).
[16] See p. 32.

sixteen volumes to each of ten poor vicarages in the diocese of Carlisle, 'the several books . . . to be kept within the church . . . for the use of the vicars there for the time being and their successors for ever.' The books thus given were (1–4) either Hammond's *Works* in four volumes, or four volumes to an equivalent value, Jackson's *Works* (three vols.) and Towerson's *Works;* also (5) Andrewes's *Sermons,* (6) Mede's *Works,* (7) Sanderson's *Sermons* and (8) his *Nine Cases of Conscience,* (9) Pearson *On the Creed,* (10) Usher's *Body of Divinity,* (11) *The Works of the Author of the Whole Duty of Man,* (12) Sparrow's *Rationale* and (13) his *Collection of Canons,* (14) Cave's *Primitive Christianity,* (15) Herbert's *Country Parson* and (16) Walton's *Lives.* These books cost £10 10s. 8d. per set of sixteen. They were duly distributed in 1687 to the churches at Ainstable, Askham, Burgh-by-Sands, Crosby-on-Eden, Crosby Ravensworth, Dalston, Dearham, Isel, Thursby and Wigton. In 1703 when Bishop Nicolson made a primary visitation of his diocese the Bishop caused the titles of the books and the articles of agreement drawn up at the time of their distribution to be entered in his journal, so that he could make careful enquiry concerning them in each of the ten parishes.[17] What he found was not very satisfactory.[18] It is not surprising that all of them have now vanished, except eight at Dalston and four at Ainstable, considering that no provision for the housing of the books had been made by Oley's executor. The appearance of the books at Isel in the eighteenth century is recorded in a draft letter from one of the rectors: 'These Books are kept in a little study along with my own; and are sufficiently distinguished from them by the manner of their Binding. For they are all bound after an uniform manner which I take to be calf dressed in imitation of Buff. They have all been letter'd on the Back with these letters B : Oley, but the lettering is so tarnished by length of time that (it) is now scarce legible.'[19] Evidently the books were then in the rectory.

8

Bray's enthusiasm for libraries is well known.[20] He was appointed rector of Sheldon, near Birmingham, in 1690, at the age of thirty-four. He took an active interest in social affairs and as a result of this, he was picked out by Henry Compton, bishop of London, 'to model the infant church of England in the province of Maryland,' and was offered the

---

[17] *Miscellany Accounts of the Diocese of Carlisle;* ed. R. S. Ferguson, for the Cumberland and Westmorland Antiquarian and Archaeological Society, 1877, pp. 7–8.
[18] *Ibid.,* pp. 7, 14, 20, 22, 74, 77, 80, 110.
[19] The letter is kept in the church safe.
[20] For Bray see *Dict. Nat. Biogr.;* E. L. Pennington, *The Reverend Thomas Bray* (Church Historical Society [U.S.A.] Publication, no. 7), 1934; G. Smith, 'Dr. Thomas Bray,' *Library Association Record,* vol. 12 (1910), pp. 242–60; H. P. Thompson, *Thomas Bray,* 1954.

position of bishop's commissary there in 1696. Before accepting, however, he seems to have investigated whether he could get sufficient clergymen to go to the colonies, and to have formed the opinion that the only
volunteers were poor men, not in a position to buy the books necessary
to keep up their education. This state of affairs Bray reported to the
bishop, and recommended that libraries were both necessary for the
well-being of the clergy going to America, and an encouragement to
them. His recommendations were accepted, and he proceeded to Maryland, where he set up a library, named the Annapolitan Library after
Princess Anne of Denmark, at Annapolis. In furtherance of his plans he
published *Proposals for the Encouragement and Promoting of Religion
and Learning in the Foreign Plantations, 1696?*, setting out a scheme for
a parochial library in every parish in America. Another book, *An Essay
towards promoting all Necessary and Useful Knowledge, both Divine
and Human In all parts of His Majesty's Dominions, both at home and
abroad*, 1697, contained proposals to the gentry and clergy for purchasing lending libraries for all the deaneries of England where the author
had also found many clergymen too poor to own books. Bray went into
details of administration, suggesting titles of books recommended, a preliminary classification scheme, the marking and care of books. It was his
suggestion that five parishes should be grouped together as a deanery
with a decanal library to serve as a lending library 'to allow (both clergy
and gentry) to carry the books to their homes,' while the parochial
libraries would form 'standing' libraries. His *Bibliotheca Parochialis*,
published in 1697, and his *Apostolick Charity*, published in 1699, were
both intended to promote his library projects. In furtherance of the same
ends and owing to the growth of his schemes, he prepared the first sketch
of the Society for Promoting Christian Knowledge, a society with the
objects of setting up libraries at home and abroad, charity schools,
missions, etc., which held its first meeting in 1699, and two years later he
obtained the charter for the Society for the Propagation of the Gospel
throughout the British Plantations. His advocacy of parochial libraries
continued throughout his life. In 1704, in *An Introductory Discourse to
Catechetical Instruction . . . in a letter to the clergy of Maryland . . .
with a preface to . . . the parochial clergy and school masters in this
Kingdom*, he wrote, 'I would recommend the having a book press with a
lock and key, fixt in the vestry, or chancel of every Church.' In 1709
Bray put out a broadsheet *Proposal for erecting Parochial Libraries in
the Meanly endow'd Cures throughout England*, the contents of which
were summarized by William Blades in the following words:
  'Many will be surprised to hear, that in England and Wales there are

above 2,000 parishes where the income is under £30, of which 1,200 are under £20, and 500 under £10. Of necessity these are without books, a deficiency which good men have often tried to supply. A committee of clergy and laity have met to promote the good work, and so far prospered that they have got together over 3,000 folios, 4,000 4tos. and 8vos., besides having put to press many books now out of print. Fifty-two libraries are now nearly complete and 500 more proposed. An Act of Parliament has been passed for the better preservation of Parochial Libraries, and those who are willing to be benefactors to this charity, are desired to pay the sum they shall contribute to Mr. Henry Hoare, in Fleet Street, London.'[21]

The Act of Parliament mentioned in this *Proposal* was passed on 4 March 1708–9.[22] The preamble includes the following passage: 'Whereas in many Places . . . the Provision for the Clergy is so mean, that the necessary Expence of Books for the better Prosecution of their Studies cannot be defrayed by them; and whereas of late Years, several charitable and well-disposed Persons have by charitable Contributions erected Libraries within several Parishes and Districts in *England* and *Wales;* but some Provision is wanting to preserve the same . . . from Embezilment; Be it therefore enacted . . . That in every Parish or Place where such a Library is or shall be erected, the same shall be preserved for such Use and Uses, as the same is and shall be given, and the Orders and Rules of the Founder and Founders of such Libraries shall be observed and kept.' The following are its main provisions:

(2) Every incumbent, rector, vicar, minister, or curate of a parish, before he shall be permitted to use and enjoy such library, shall give security for the preservation of the library and due observation of the rules and orders belonging to it.

(4) The incumbent shall make a catalogue of the library to be delivered to the ordinary.

(5) Where a library is already erected, the catalogue shall be ready before 29 September 1709, or in the case of a new library, within six months of its foundation.

(6) Upon the death of an incumbent, the library shall be locked up by the churchwardens.

(8) The incumbent shall enter the names of benefactors in a book.

(10) Books shall not be alienated without the consent of the ordinary, and then only if they are duplicates.

[21] Quoted from Blades's preface to the reprint (1889) of *An Overture for Founding and Maintaining of Bibliothecks in every Paroch throughout this Kingdom* (i.e. Scotland), a pamphlet printed in 1699 and attributed to James Kirkwood, minister of Minto.
[22] For the full text of the Act see below, p. 48.

9

Some of the information given in Bray's *Proposal* and in the Act may have been based on the replies to a printed Advertisement by 'a Divine of the Church of England' inserted at the foot of a broadsheet royal Brief. The Brief, dated 28 February 1704–5, was issued to raise money, 'upwards of £4,800,' for the rebuilding of All Saints' Church, Oxford.[23] The Advertisement is addressed, 'To the Reverend the Minister of every Parochial Church and Chapel in England.' Bray himself replied to it as minister of Sheldon. It asks ten questions. Ministers were requested to answer them on the back or at the foot of the Advertisement. Question 6 is, 'What library is settled or settling in your Parish, and by whom?' Question 7 is, 'If the yearly Value of your Rectory, Vicarage, or Chappelry be under £30, how much?' On the return of the Briefs 1579 replies to the Advertisement were detached. They now form the document known as 'Notitia Parochialis.'[24]

Nearly all the incumbents who replied to the Advertisement either did not answer question 6 or said that there was no library settled or settling in their parish. Thirty-one of them gave positive answers, saying that they had or were getting a library (23), or that there was a school library (2) or a town library (1), or some other sort of library (2) in the parish, or referring to individual books in possession of the incumbents for ever (3).[25] What they have to say is often of interest to us. It was, no doubt, of interest to Bray and his friends.

10

The Committee of laity and clergy to which Bray referred in his *Proposal* and of which he was a member was a Committee of the Society for

[23] A copy of the Brief and Advertisement returned from Gotham, Nottinghamshire, without contribution to the fund or a reply to the Advertisement, is now Bodleian MS. Rawlinson B.407a f. 144.

[24] Lambeth Palace MSS. 960–5. The replies were bound up in these six volumes by A. C. Ducarel, Lambeth Librarian. He had bought them in 1760 from the Revd. Mr. Entick of Stepney, who had bought them in the Harleian sale.

[25] The 'Notitia Parochialis' contains information about the following libraries included in the alphabetical list on pp. 63–107 of this publication: Beccles, Bicester, Bilston, Bury (Lancashire), Chirbury, Costock, Denchworth, Frisby-on-the-Wreak, Hull (S. Mary Lowgate), Hurley, Leicester, Nantwich, Newcastle-upon-Tyne, North Grimston, Reigate, Sheffield, Sheldon, Skipton, Sleaford, Stainton, Warwick, Womersley, York (S. Mary Castlegate): and also about school libraries at Cheltenham and at Newport, Shropshire (nos. 1485, 1311); about a library in the town at Gainsborough 'settling by the voluntary Subscriptions of several persons which was begun A.D. 1696' (no. 879); about a library at Bishops Castle, Shropshire: 'We have no public library, only a private one for the use of neighbors given by Charles Mason Esq. one of oʳ Representatives in Parliament' (no. 358); about the library in the collegiate (and parochial) church of Southwell 'settling by yᵉ Prebendaries and Neighbouring Gentlemen, but it advances slowly' (no. 1252); and about individual books at Myndtown, Shropshire—'but one book of Dr. Braye's gift'—(no. 418); at Crosthwaite, Cumberland, a Josephus in Greek and Latin given by Mr. Appleford of S. John's College, Cambridge (no. 1182); and at Greenford, Middlesex, Walton's *Polyglot* and Castell's *Lexicon*, donor unknown (no. 546). The other libraries founded before 1705 (see pp. 42–3) were in parishes from which no reply to the advertisement was made, except Halifax (no. 397), whose incumbent did not answer the question about the library.

Promoting Christian Knowledge. It functioned from 1705 until 1729. Henry Newman, the able secretary of S.P.C.K., was also secretary of the Committee, and its activities are set out in his admirable minutes and in the full record of correspondence which he kept. The Minute Book, called 'The Proceedings of the Trustees for Erecting Parochial Librarys; and Promoting Other Charitable Designs,' the correspondence, and the accounts preserved at S.P.C.K. Headquarters reveal the care with which the Committee furthered its scheme. They reveal also that important as Bray was as a promoter of parochial libraries, it is wrong to say, as has commonly been said, that he himself founded them. The sixty-four or more libraries established between 1710 and 1729 were the Committee's libraries. On the Committee two men of substance, Henry Hoare, and Robert Nelson, were in their way no less vital than Bray to its success.[26] Contributions received on fifty occasions in the years 1706 to 1710 amounted to £1,738 8s.[27]

The first meeting of the Committee was on 30 July 1705. The minutes of this meeting begin with the words 'Whereas the Reverend Dr Bray has communicated to Sr Humphrey Mackworth, Mr Nelson, Mr Hoar, and Mr Brewster a Proposal for encouraging and erecting Parochial and Lending Libraries.'[28] The Committee soon decided that parochial libraries, permanent and inalienable, were to be preferred to lending libraries.[28a] 'A Catalogue of Books suitable for a Parochial Catechetick Librarie' was produced at the meeting on 8 March 1705–6. Thereafter four years were spent in preparing libraries for despatch. At first the foundation of not less than 500 libraries was thought of, but the number was soon reduced to fifty-two, approximately two to each diocese. The first two libraries were sent to Evesham and Henley-in-Arden in March 1710. In all twenty-two were sent out in 1710, fifteen in 1711, and fourteen in 1712.[29] The fifty-second library was sent to Oldbury in August 1713. With one exception,[30] each of these fifty-two libraries consisted of either seventy-two or sixty-seven volumes,[31] and cost with binding, travelling cupboard, and carriage, between £21 10s. and £22 11s. Of this sum, £5 was required from the incumbent of each parish to which a library was sent.[32] The rest was defrayed by the Committee.

[26] See p. 30.
[27] Minutes of Library Committee 1705—1729–30, *ad. fin.*
[28] Minutes, p. 1.
[28a] Cf. p. 20.
[29] See p. 44.
[30] See p. 64 (Alcester).
[31] See p. 34.
[32] The £5 was sometimes paid by a benefactor. Thus Sir Thomas Lowther appears to have paid for Flookburgh (see p. 31) and Mr. Wentworth of Wentworth Woodhouse for Bolsterstone, Harrowden Parva, Irthlingborough, Tinsley, Wentworth, and Wollaston (Bodleian MS. Rawlinson D. 834, f. 6).

After the completion of its immediate task the Committee continued to function, but with less vigour. Enough books were collected and bound to allow the despatch of eight libraries, numbered 55–62,[33] in 1720 and 1721. No. 63 went to Flookburgh in 1725 and no. 64 to Shustoke in 1727. In 1729 preparations for ten more libraries were made and two libraries seem to have been sent to St. Mary's in the Scilly Isles and to Burwell in Cambridgeshire.[34] The one hundred and tenth and last meeting of the Committee was on 3 March 1730, a fortnight after Bray's death. Subsequently a new body was formed, The Associates of the late Reverend Dr. Bray. The Associates founded seventy-three small parochial libraries between 1757 and 1768, mainly in North Lancashire and Wales. Later their foundations were, as they still are, lending libraries.

The Associates stopped founding parochial libraries at about the time when there is a marked falling off in the number of parochial libraries founded by individuals, and when the question about parochial libraries ceased to be put to the clergy at visitations. The present alphabetical list refers to six permanent libraries founded by individuals in the 1780s and 1790s, and to nine permanent libraries founded by individuals in the nineteenth century. Some of these latter libraries contain a fair number of pre-1800 books. Others like the collection at Myddle founded by Lord Bridgewater and now on deposit at Shrewsbury Public Library, and the collection at All Saints, Eastbourne, are entirely nineteenth century and have been omitted from the list. The library at Finedon founded in 1788 was 'for the sole use of the Ministers of Finedon for ever, the Foundation Book being Dr Thomas Bray's *Bibliotheca Parochialis*.' A century later the gifts to Prees (1883) and Eastbourne (1890) have the same restricted use. On the other hand, the libraries at Elham (1809) and Castleton (1819) were for the use of the parish, and the library at Bewdley (1819) was for the clergy and 'respectable inhabitants' of the town and neighbourhood. The library at S. Peter's-in-the-East, Oxford (1841) is of special interest as an 'Oxford Movement' library. On the whole the learned character of the libraries was maintained in these nineteenth-century foundations, and in the additions made at this time to the few older libraries which had funds at their disposal, for example, Holy Trinity, Hull.

By 1849 when the Select Committee on Public Libraries was taking

---

[33] The libraries sent to Virginia and Montserrat were numbered 53 and 54.

[34] Minutes, pp. 167–70. The libraries sent (about this time?) to How in Norfolk 'at the request of Lady Betty Hastings' and to Streatley in Bedfordshire are known only from catalogues found recently by the Revd. H. P. Thompson among loose papers belonging to the Associates of Dr. Bray.

evidence and preparing its Report, many of the old libraries were suffering from neglect and had fallen into disuse. The Select Committee in its Report depended largely on the evidence of Edward Edwards and the Revd. J. J. Smith. It noted that 'Parochial Libraries once prevailed to a considerable extent throughout England, Wales and Scotland. . . . Their foundation was, in the first instance, due to individual benevolence; but subsequently and principally, to the efforts of Dr. Bray and his "Associates," at the beginning, and in the middle, of the last century. They were generally intended for the use of the clergy. . . . Of many of these Libraries, it is stated that "the books lie exposed to chance, and liable to be torn by the children of the village." In one, however, that of Beccles, in Suffolk, the books have been rescued from danger. They have been deposited in a room in the town, and "made the commencement of a Town Library." Your Committee cannot but recommend that the example of the people of Beccles should be imitated whenever there is an existing parish library.'[35]

Possibly arising out of this Report there was a considerable correspondence about parochial libraries in the pages of *Notes and Queries* in the years 1852–9. William Blades listed many of them under the heading 'Minor Libraries' in *The Bookworm* for 1866, and in 1879 another list was prepared by T. W. Shore at a conference of the newly formed Library Association.

The renewed interest in the fabric of churches extended sometimes to their libraries. From time to time during the last century and a quarter individuals have described them, catalogued them, and cared for them. There are particularly good descriptions in print of Denchworth (1875), Doncaster (1882), King's Lynn (1904), Tiverton (1905), Marlborough (1947) and of the libraries in Lancashire.[36] At least forty-four church libraries have been catalogued in print since 1820, if sometimes very badly catalogued. Jacob Ley had the books at Wendlebury rebound at his own expense in 1840. G. J. French restored the chained library at Turton in the fifties, and the library at Henley was put in order and labelled at about the same time. Canon Fletcher made Wimborne the model library it now is during the time that he was vicar there. We owe the continued existence of the interesting library at Marlborough largely to Mr. E. G. H. Kempston. In recent years the libraries at Langley Marish, Maldon, and Reigate have been assisted by the Pilgrim Trustees. Maldon and Reigate are receiving annual County Council grants.

[35] *Reports from Committees*, 1849, pp. vi, vii.
[36] R. C. Christie, *The old Church and School Libraries of Lancashire*, Chetham Society, New Series, vol. 7, (1885).

D

Neglect, not care, is, however, the usual story. Many libraries have vanished mysteriously, some of them, like Brent Eleigh and Northampton, in the not very distant past. In many, the books have become gradually less in number. Libraries at Broughton, Durham, Effingham, Flaxley, London (S. George the Martyr, Queen Square, and S. Martin-in-the-Fields), Manchester, Milden, Norton-cum-Lenchwick, Reepham, Royston, Shipdham, Stanground, and Whitchurch (Hampshire) have been sold: of these the S. Martin's, Shipdham, and Whitchurch collections were important. Libraries at Coniston, Hillingdon, Llanrhos, Milton Abbas, North Walsham, and Wendlebury, and parts of libraries at Bushey, Lanteglos-by-Camelford, Mentmore, and Steeple Ashton, have been destroyed deliberately. Libraries at Doncaster, Liverpool, and Willen, and part of the library at Great Yarmouth, have been destroyed by the accidents of war and fire. Probably the neglect of books kept in dry conditions has been harmless, but damp has caused damage at, for example, Bury St. Edmunds and Norton (Derbyshire).

12

The neglect is understandable. By the second half of the eighteenth century the permanent parochial library founded by an individual with his own books was beginning to be out of fashion. People who wished to read beyond their own shelves and could afford the money were able in many places to subscribe to a lending-library of modern books. Libraries of this sort were formed under various auspices, often not ecclesiastical, in at least most towns, and in many villages. At Witham and perhaps at Caerleon and Llanbadarn Fawr a church lending-library was founded before 1800.[37] At Bridgnorth and at Stockton-on-Tees, the old parochial library was turned into a subscription library in the nineteenth century, increased in size, and for a time flourished. The parochial library founded at Bromfield in Cumberland in the middle of the nineteenth century may be taken as an example of a subscription library under church patronage. The Bishop of Carlisle was patron and all parishioners subscribing one shilling annually were members. There were about one thousand volumes and one hundred and ninety-two subscribing parishioners in 1853, when a catalogue was printed.[38] The intention was—in the words of the Address prefixed to the catalogue—not only 'to open to the Parishioners at large the sources of innocent gratification which properly

[37] The books in the parochial and lending libraries founded by the Associates of Dr. Bray from 1753 onwards (see p. 24 and *Life and Designs of Thomas Bray,* ed. 1808, pp. 81–3) did not belong to the parish to which they were sent, but remained the property of the Associates, returnable if no longer required.

[38] *A Catalogue of the Bromfield Parochial Library,* Wigton, 1853. A copy to which Mr. G. K. Scott drew attention is in the Public Library, Carlisle.

directed Reading is capable of affording, but also to offer the means of self-instruction to those, who might have but few other opportunities for the improvement of the mind.' No doubt many other libraries with these aims were founded at this time. In 1873, at a visitation of the diocese of Canterbury more than half the incumbents answered the question 'Have you a library in your parish?' in the affirmative.[39] These libraries were useful, especially in country districts, in the days before County Library services existed, but most of them have disappeared without leaving any trace of their existence. They do not concern us here.[40]

13

Book-rooms, furniture, and chains. Research on parochial libraries suggests that nothing has been so important to them as a good home. Their founders were often aware of this and prepared special rooms for the safe keeping of the books. Some of these rooms still exist as at Hatfield Broad Oak and Langley Marish. Others, as at Denchworth, Henley, and Rougham were destroyed during alterations to the church, leaving the library homeless. In many churches the room over the south porch was a ready-made library-room; in some there was a room over the vestry fit for the purpose. These upper-storey libraries are often charming. They are attractive even when neglected. They are as a rule dry and the books in them, on shelving against the walls, have often kept well, with no greater enemy than dust. It is easy to think of them as happy summer refuges for the married clergy.

The best known libraries now are the chained libraries. People with no interest in old books are prepared to be interested in chains. Wimborne, Grantham, and Hereford (All Saints) have many visitors. The two first are doubly attractive, being chained in an upper room.

In parsonages, 'standing' libraries have not been happy as a rule. To Heathfield in Sussex a wise founder left not only the books in 'my press,' but also the press itself 'for ever to be kept in a dry convenient place in the Vicarage House.' Books and press are still there. In most other parsonages the books have probably been eyed with disfavour by one or more in the long series of incumbents. They have tended to find their way to an attic, if not to an outhouse or a sale room. The sale or subdivision of over-large parsonages has not made them more secure in recent times.

[39] The Returns are in the library of Lambeth Palace.

[40] Incumbents replying to a questionnaire sent out by the Central Council for the Care of Churches in 1950 referred to modern libraries in active use at S. Olave's, York, S. Martin's, Hull, and Westcliff-on-Sea (Essex), to the specialist collection of liturgical books at Wellingborough, and to the local collection housed in the 'scriptorium' at Selby Abbey.

Most of the libraries included in the alphabetical list, and still *in situ,* fall, as to their placing, into one of four divisions. They are in an upper room, or the vestry, or the body of a church, or in the parsonage.[41]

(i) *In the upper room of a church.* Ashby-de-la-Zouch, Astley, Bloxham, Boston, Bromham, Broughton, Chelmsford, Finedon, Grantham, Loughborough, More, Nantwich, Newark, Newport (Essex), Ottery St. Mary, Oxford, Reigate, St. Neots, Stoke-by-Nayland, Swaffham, Wimborne, Wotton-under-Edge.

(ii) *In the vestry.* Amberley, Bassingbourne, Beccles, Bradfield, Bury St. Edmunds, Cartmel, Hackness, Hatfield Broad Oak, Hull (S. Mary Lowgate), Kildwick, Stamford, Tiverton, Tong, Woodbridge.

(iii) *In the body of a church.* Denchworth, Feckenham, Hereford (All Saints: in the Lady Chapel, which was formerly a vestry), Oakham.

(iv) *In the parsonage.* Ainstable, Bampton, Chirbury, Coddenham, Cole Orton (at present in store), Crundale,[42] Dalston, Darowen, Doddington, Donington, East Harlsey, Heathfield, Lanteglos-by-Camelford, Lawshall, Plymtree, Steeple Ashton, Tortworth, Whitchurch (Salop), Woodchurch, Worsborough, Yelden. Cf. Effingham, Norton-cum-Lenchwick.

At Halton, King's Cliffe, and Maldon, the library is in a special building apart from church and parsonage. At Leicester in 1632 and at Brent Eleigh in 1859 the library was moved from the church to a building specially constructed for it in the churchyard. At Bicester, Chirbury, and King's Norton, the library was attached to a grammar school in close proximity to the church.

Thirty-five libraries formerly in churches or parsonages have been moved elsewhere since 1800.

Alnwick	to Newcastle Cathedral Library
Ash	to Kent County Library, Maidstone
Barnstable	to Roborough Library, Exeter University
Bath	to Bath Public Library
Bedford	to Bedford Public Library
Bewdley	to Birmingham University Library
Birmingham	to Birmingham Public Library
Bolton	to Bolton School
Broughton (part)	to Cambridge University Library
Bushey	to the Community of the Resurrection, Mirfield
Elham (part)	to Canterbury Cathedral Library
Elston	to Nottinghamshire County Library

[41] The following lists do not aim at completeness.
[42] Now at Godmersham Vicarage.

Grantham (Newcome collection) to Grantham Public Library
Graveley   to Jesus College, Cambridge
Great Yarmouth   to Great Yarmouth Public Library (temporarily)
Henley-on-   to Reading University Library and to Christ
    Thames   Church, Oxford
Hull (Holy
    Trinity)   to Hull University Library
King's Lynn (part) to King's Lynn Public Library
King's Norton   to Birmingham Public Library
Liverpool   to Church House, Liverpool (destroyed)
Shoreditch
 (London)   to Shoreditch Central Library, Hoxton
Maidstone   to Maidstone Museum
Marlborough   to Marlborough College
Martock   to Wells Cathedral
Mentmore   to Bucks Archaeological Society, Aylesbury
Newcastle (Thomlinson collection) to Newcastle Public Library
Norton   to Sheffield Public Library
Prees   to County Record Office, Shrewsbury
Salford   to Salford Public Library
Shipdham (residue unsold) to Norwich Public Library
Skipton   to Skipton Public Library
Spalding   to the Spalding Gentlemen's Society
Stainton   to York Minster Library
Stonehouse   to Stonehouse Secondary Modern School
Tankersley   to York Minster Library
Warwick (part)   to Warwick County Record Office
Wisbech   to Wisbech Museum

II. THE S.P.C.K. LIBRARIES, 1705–29[1]

1. LETTERS FROM HENRY NEWMAN, SECRETARY OF S.P.C.K.

F O U R letters written by Henry Newman in the summer of 1725 are of particular interest. In two of them Newman informed his correspondent, Thomas Sharp, rector of Rothbury and archdeacon of Northumberland, about the Committee and its aims. The other two illustrate the whole business of sending out a library, that sent to Flookburgh in North Lancashire which still remains in the church there. Extracts from the two letters to Sharp will suffice:

Letter 1 (extract). Newman to Sharp, Middle Temple, 27 May 1725[2]
In answer to yours of the 21st Curr^t the Design of Parochial Libraries is still carry'd on, but with less Vigour than it us'd to be when Mr Nelson, and Mr Henry Hoare were living, who were great Benefactors to it out of their own Pockets.[3]

I have Part of the Material for 20 Libraries by me, upon the same Model as those already sent out, 10 of which are far advanced; and, if Mr Hoare had liv'd, I believe, would have been compleated this Summer, but now I don't know when they may be compleated, unless kind Providence should raise up some Friend to the Undertaking like those I mentioned.

If You please to signify the Name of the Place You would recommend for a Library, and who will engage for the Payment of the Five Pound Præmium, when a Library can be had, I will take Care to recommend it to the Gentlemen concern'd in Promoting this Charity at their next Meeting.

I must acquaint You with the Qualifications expected in ye Livings where these Libraries are bestow'd. Viz^t

That they do not exceed £30 per Annum, certain Value to the Incumbent; And that the Incumbent be resident, and give Bond, with the Penalty of £30. to the Bishop of the Diocese for observing the Rules prescrib'd by Act of Parliament and the Founders.

[1] See pp. 18–24.
[2] Archives of S.P.C.K., EL. 1 CS/1, p. 201. This and the other letters are in the hand of Newman's clerk.
[3] For Robert Nelson, 1665–1715, see *Dict. Nat. Biogr.* Henry Hoare, died in March 1725, aged 48, and bequeathed large sums to various charities: see J. Wilford, *Memorials and Characters*, 1741, p. 778. He suggested the inclusion of Bishop Beveridge's *Private Thoughts* in the libraries and paid for the fifty-two copies bought by the Committee (Minutes, 1705–30, p. 58).

Letter 2 (extract). Newman to Sharp, Middle Temple, 17 July 1725[4]

At first the Gentlemen concerned did indeed propose the placing of 2. Libraries in each Diocese, as a Specimen of the Charity they intended, but they soon found themselves oblig'd to break thrô that Design; some Bishops entertaining the Proposal very coldly, while others were very eager in Promoting it, among the last of which was the late excellent Arch-Bishop Sharp, and his Successor, and therefore there are as many Libraries of this kind in your Diocese as in any two Dioceses in the Kingdom, except Worcester, the late Bishop of which was a zealous Promoter of them.[5]

Letter 3. Newman to Richard Hudson, curate of Flookburgh, 'in Cartmell, near Lancaster,' Middle Temple, 12 June 1725[6]

Rev[d] Sir,

Yesterday there was deliver'd to M[r] Knowles Jun[r], the Lancaster Carrier, a Parochial Library for yo[r] Chappel at Flookborough, in 2 Cases, cover'd with Matts, and directed to You.

They are a Present to yo[r] Chappel from some Gentlemen who are Founders of several Parochial Libraries, and, at the Desire of Sir Thomas Lowther, who has been a Benefactor to the Undertaking, this Library is sent to You, in Hopes You will take due Care of it, as the Rules direct, so that the Books may be all safely transmitted to yo[r] Successor. I have sent, in the least Case, 2. Catologues, with a Receipt endors'd, which you are desir'd to sign in the Presence of Your Church-Wardens, or other noted Inhabitants in your Parish or Neighbourhood, and to send one them (*sic*) to your Diocesan, and the other when sign'd to me, under Cover to Sir Thomas Lowther in Red Lion Street.

The Key of both Cases is fasten'd to the under Part of the Least Case under the Matt.

Sir Thomas Lowther desires You would give Directions for conveying y[e] Cases from Lancaster to Flookborough, at the first of which Places M[r] Knowles has promis'd to deliver it next Monday Sennight, to which Place also, i.e. Lancaster, the Carriage is paid here.

Pray let me hear from You assoon as You receive the Library if not before, because I am to fill up a Bond, in the Bishop's Name, in the Penalty of £30. only, which You are to execute, as all the Security the Founders require of You, that You will not embezzle or destroy the

[4] EL. 1 CS/1, p. 205.
[5] Bishop Lloyd of Worcester contributed books to the value of £30 in 1706 (Minutes, 1705–30, p. 5).
[6] EL. 1 CS/1, p. 203.

Books, but preserve them as the Act of Parliament, and the Rules of the Founders prescribe for your own Use, and the Use of Your Successor.

I wish them safe to You, and am,

Revd Sir,

Your most humble Servant

Henry Newman.

You will see the Form of the Bond which You are to execute in the Register which accompanies the Library.

Letter 4. Newman to Hudson, Middle Temple, 13 July 1725 [7]

Reverend Sir,

I have Yours of the 24th past under Cover to Sir Thomas Lowther, with the Catalogue of the Library sign'd; and as You make no Complaint of the Books not being in good Order, I hope they were carefully deliver'd.

I herewith send the Bond, which You are to sign and execute in presence of Your Church-Warden and principal Parishioners, which, when done, I must desire You to send under Sir Thomas Lowther's Cover to me: for thô it be taken in the Bishop's Name, I am to lay it before the Founders of the Library for their Directions to transmit it to the Bishop of the Diocese, but the other Catalogue, which I sent to You, You are desir'd to send to his Lordship, as mention'd in my Letter of the 12th of last Month.

I wish You may long enjoy the Effect of Sir Thomas's Kindness to You, which must be an agreable Companion to a Man of Letters destitute of Books in a Solitary Country, and, if rightly used, must enable You to do more good, as a Minister of the Gospel, to feed with Heavenly Truths the Flock committed to your Care.

Please to let me know where they are plac'd, whether in the Vestry or your dwelling House, that I may be able to inform the Founders thereof being,

Revd Sir,

Your most humble Servant

Henry Newman

2. BOOKS, BOOK-PLATES, CATALOGUES, CUPBOARDS, AND BONDS

The surviving books, book-plates, catalogues, book-cupboards, and bonds illustrate the matters referred to in the Minutes and Accounts and in Newman's letters.

[7] EL. 1 CS/1, p. 204.

(a) Bridlington Priory, Yorkshire: an eighteenth century book case designed for the S.P.C.K. library founded there in 1710. A list of the books and a copy of the Act of Queen Anne can be seen inside the open cupboard door. The books were placed in the cupboard specially for this photograph; normally they are kept elsewhere in the church.

[Photo: Foster Brigham.

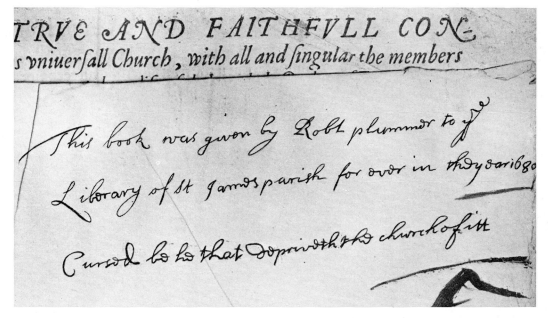

[Photo: F. E. Williams.

(b) An ill-written but apt inscription in a copy of Foxe's Book of Martyrs in Bury St. Edmunds Cathedral Library (formerly parochial) which reads 'This book was given by Robt. Plummer to ye Liberary of St. James parish for ever in the year 1680. Cursed be he that depriveth the church of itt.'

PLATE I

[*Photo: Robert Lee.*

(*a*) Press inscribed 'The Gift of Humphrey Chetham 1655' with drop lid forming a writing or reading desk. The home of the Chetham Library in Gorton parish church, Lancs.

[*Photo: National Buildings Record.*

(*b*) The library of some 200 books at All Saints', Hereford, is housed in the Lady Chapel (formerly the vestry). The books were nearly sold to America in 1870.

[*Photo: Rev. P. S. Thon*

(*c*) Chained copy of Bp. Jewel's *Defense of the Apologie the Church of Englande* 1571, with the contemporary lect which was probably made to hold it at Great Durnford, W

PLATE II

A. *The books and their bindings.* Substantial remains of ten of the sixty-two libraries founded between 1705 and 1727 still exist. They are at Bridlington, Darlington, Darowen, Dudleston, Feckenham (nearly complete), Flookburgh, Poulton, Preston-by-Wingham, and St. Neots, and, transferred from Newport (Mon.), at Llandaff Cathedral.[8] Other libraries existed into the nineteenth century, but from 1868 onwards the secretary of the Associates of Dr. Bray made strenuous and on the whole successful efforts to secure the return of old books: 'Our great object is to get rid of the libraries which are useless and at least of all the useless books out of libraries which the Clergy value.'[9] Many of the clergy objected to this policy,[10] which should have been applied, if at all, only to libraries founded by the Associates themselves and not to the older and inalienable parochial libraries founded by the Committee of S.P.C.K. The North Walsham library was dispersed as recently as 1938.

The books still surviving *in situ* are mostly in good condition and are almost without exception in their original calf bindings, plain except for small corner-ornaments.[11] The accounts show that the Committee first employed John Worall as their binder, then F. Fox, and finally and chiefly Philip Cholmondeley. The books they bound are named individually. Thus Worall was paid £8 5s. for binding fifty-two copies of Eusebius in 1709 and Cholmondeley was paid £2 7s. 8d. for binding fifty-two copies of Placette and Godeau in 1710.[12]

B. *Book-plates.* A book-plate was placed in each volume sent out and is still to be found in most of the books in the existing libraries. The plate in the larger books shows S. John on Patmos and an angel giving him a book with the words 'Accipe Librum et devora illum' (Revelation 10 : 9): the book-cupboard shown in this design is an accurate reproduction of the cupboard in which the books actually travelled from London. The plate in the smaller books shows a kneeling figure and is inscribed 'Tolle Lege' and 'Vid.S^{ti} Aug. Confess. Lib. 8 Cap. 12.'[13] Both plates were printed in 1709 from copper-plates designed by Simon Gribelin. The 'Accounts 1706–11,' ff. 6^v, 8^v, and the Minutes, pp. 52–3, where speci-

[8] For details see the Alphabetical List under these places, and also for a few surviving books, Alnwick, Newport (Essex) and Lostwithiel.
[9] The quotation is from a letter lying loose at p. 134 of a manuscript volume of 'Review Papers' belonging to the Associates, dated 1868–75.
[10] See Alphabetical List, Corston.
[11] On forty-four books at Bridlington there seem to be fifteen different corner-ornaments and on forty books at Darlington eleven different corner-ornaments, three of which are different from any of those at Bridlington.
[12] Accounts, 1706–11.
[13] Reproduced in the annual report of the Associates for 1944 and some other years after 1944.

E

mens of the book-plates are inserted, record that 8,000 copies were printed.

The Franks Collection of Book-plates in the British Museum contains examples of the plates from books formerly in S.P.C.K. libraries at Evesham, Henley-in-Arden, and Tinsley (nos. 33850, 33854, 33865).

C. *Catalogues.* (i) Shelf-catalogues of each of the fifty-two libraries sent out in the years 1710 to 1713 are to be found in a single volume now belonging to the Associates, who received it as a gift from S.P.C.K. The catalogues show that the stocks of books assembled by the Committee were made up into thirty-two identical libraries, each of seventy-two volumes, and into twenty substantially identical libraries, each normally of sixty-seven volumes.[14] Each library was given a reference number from 1 to 52 and this number was written at the head of the catalogue. The numbers bear no relation to the order in which the libraries were sent out. (ii) One volume in each library was called 'The Register.' The surviving 'Registers' of Alnwick (now at Newcastle), Corston, Preston-by-Wingham, Darlington, Trevethin, North Walsham, and Wollaston (now in the Bodleian) are vellum-covered blank-books of about eighty-five leaves, containing a catalogue of the books, and in front of the catalogue printed copies of the *Proposal for erecting Parochial Libraries in the Meanly endow'd Cures throughout England,*[15] of the Act of 7 Anne 'for the better Preservation of Parochial Libraries,' and of 'Rules for the better Preservation of Parochial Libraries.'[16] Most of the leaves remain blank. (iii) Besides the 'Register' two catalogues were sent with each library. They were to be signed by the incumbent in the presence of witnesses and returned by him, one to his bishop and the other to the secretary of S.P.C.K. The catalogues returned to Newman from Over Whitacre, Chepstow, Oldbury, Whitchurch, and Malton are now in the Bodleian, MS. Rawlinson D. 834 ff. 13–14, 20–1, 24–5, 31, 34.

The catalogue of the library sent to Oldbury is here printed from the Bodleian manuscript, ff. 24–5, as a specimen of the seventy-two volume library sent to the incumbents of thirty-two churches: Brewood, *Bridlington,* Bolsterstone, Brookthorpe, Chepstow, *Darlington,* Detling, *Dudleston,* Dullingham, Elmley, *Feckenham,* Flaxley, Irthlingborough, Kilmersdon, Kingsbridge, Llanbadarn Fawr, Llanrhos (Eglws Rhôs), Lostwithiel, Marske, Monmouth, Newport (Essex), *Newport* (Mon.), Oldbury, Oundle, Over Whitacre, Oxenhall, Prendergast, *St. Neots,* Slapton, Tinsley, Trevethin, and Wollaston.[17]

---

[14] Sixty-six volumes at Kirkoswald and St. Bees; seventy-four volumes at Alcester.
[15] See p. 20.
[16] The Act (see p. 48) and the Rules are printed in the *Life and Designs of Thomas Bray,* ed. 1808, pp. 69–75.   [17] Italics show the surviving libraries.

A CATALOGUE of the Parochial Library at OLDBURY
in Shropshire N°. 38

Diocese of Worcester		I. SHELF	£	s	d
1		The Ecclesiastical History of Eusebius &c	1		
2		A :Bp. Tillotson's Works in folio 7. Edit.		18	
3, 4		Dr. Whitby's Commentary on the New Testament 2. Vol.	1	15	
5		Chillingworth's Works		12	
6	Bound	Dr. Bray's Catechetical Lectures		8	
		Allen's Discourse on the two Covenants		2	
7	Bound	Allen's Discourse on Faith		8	
		Kettlewell's Practical Believer			
8		Bp. Pearson's Exposition of the Creed		10	
9		The Register		4	
10		Dr. More's Theological Works	1	1	6
			6	18	6

		II. SHELF			
11		A.Bp. Leighton's Comment. on part of the 1st. Epistle of S. Peter		5	
12, 13		Reeve's Translation of the Apol. of Iustin Martyr; Tertullian and Minutius Fælix &c. with the Commonit. of Vinc. Lirin. 2. Vol.		9	
14		Dr. Bray's Bibliotheca Parochialis		4	
15	Bound	Placette's christian Casuist		5	
		Godeau's Pastoral Instructions			
16–20		Dr. Scotts' Christian Life in 5. Vol.	1	1	
21		Ostervald's Causes of Corruption among christians		5	
22		—— of Uncleaness		3	6
23–4		Bp. Beveridge's Sermons the two first Vol.		8	
25		Howell's Discourse on the Lord's Day		4	
26		Bp. Stillingfleet's Vindication of the Doctrine of the Trinity		3	6
27		Dr. Goodman's Penitent Pardon'd		4	
28		—— Winter Evening Conferences		3	6
29		Reform'd Devotions published by Dr. Hickes		3	
30		Grotius de Veritate Religionis Christianæ		2	6
31		Dr. Lucas's Practical Christianity		3	
32		Bp. King's Inventions of Men in the Worship of God		1	
			4	5	

IIId. SHELF

				£	s	d
33	A : Bp. Tillotson of Sincerity in Religion	15. Sermons			4	
34	Ditto's Posthum. Sermons on several Subjects	16. Serm.	2. Vol.		4	
35	Ditto	16. Serm.	3. Vol.		4	
36	Ditto	15. Serm.	4. Vol.		4	
37	Ditto	13. Serm.	5. Vol.		4	
38	Ditto on the Attributes of God	14. Serm.	6. Vol.		4	
39	Ditto on Ditto	15. Serm.	7. Vol.		4	
40	Ditto on Repentance	15. Serm.	8. Vol.		4	
41	Ditto on Death, Iudgemt. & future State	15. Serm.	9. Vol.		4	
42	Ditto on the Life, Sufferings &c. of Christ and the coming of the Holy Ghost	15. Serm.	10. Vol.		4	
43	Ditto on several Subjects	15. Serm.	11. Vol.		4	
44	Ditto	15. Serm.	12. Vol.		4	
45	Ditto on the Truth of the Christian Religion	15. Serm.	13. Vol.		4	
46	Ditto on several Subjects	6. Serm.	14. Vol.		4	
47	Kettlewell on the Sacrament				3	6
48	Ditto's Measures of Christian Obedience				5	
49	Bishop Burnett's Abridgement of the History of the Reformation				5	
50	Dr. Gastrell's Christian Institutes				3	6
51	Bound { Bp. Beveridge's private Thoughts / Publick Prayer / frequent Communion }				5	

	£	s	d
	3	18	

IVth. SHELF

		£	s	d
52, 53	Jenkins's Certainty of the christian Religion in 2. Vols.		9	
54	Nelson's Feasts and Fasts of the Church of England		5	
55	Bp. Stillingfleet concerning Christ's Satisfaction		5	
56	Dr. Comber of Ordination		5	
57	Wheatly's Harmony and Excellency of the Common Prayer		3	
58	Bennett's Abridgement of the London Cases		3	6
59	Confutation of Popery		3	6
60	Confutation of Quakerism		3	6

61		Bp. Wilkins's Natural Religion	4	6
62		Dr. Cave's Primitive Christianity	5	
63	Bound	Dr. Hickes's Apolog. Vindic. of the Church of England	2	
		Bp. Ken's Exposition on the Church Catechism	1	
64	Bound	Dr. Worthington on self Resignation	2	6
		Spinckes of Trust in God	3	
65		Bonnel's Life	2	6
66	Bound	Dr. Bray's Catechetical Institution / Baptismal Covenant / Pastoral Discourse to Young Persons	5	
67	Bound	Short Method with the Deists and Iews	2	6
		Stearne de Visitatione Infirmorum	1	
68	Bound	Dr. Clark's three practical Essays	1	
		Wall's Conference about Infant Baptism	1	
69	Bound	Herbert's Country Parson	1	6
		The Country Parson's Advice to his Parishioners	1	6
70	Bound	Allen's Discourse on Divine Assistance	1	6
		Harrison's Exposition of the church Catechism	1	6
71		Kettlewell on Death	2	
72	Bound	Io. Elis Articulor. 39 Eccl. Angl. Defensio	1	6
		Thomæ a Kempis de Imitatione Christi	1	6

3 19 6

£ s d

Brought from Shelf 1st.		6 18 6	
Ditto	2	4 5	
Ditto	3	3 18	
Ditto	4	3 19 6	
The Case		1 5	
Packing, Carryage &c of Incidental Charges		1 5	

21 11 –

Received the withinmention'd Parochial Library into my
Custody, which I promise to keep safe for the Benefit
of myself and my Successors pursuant to the Rules prescrib'd
by the Act of Parliament and the Founders, I say receiv'd
this Third day of September : 1714

In presence of   per Me Edward Hale   Curate

Tho : Pearsall junr. }
Jonathan Carpenter } of the Parish of Halesowen [1]

---

[1] The receipt is written on the otherwise blank fourth page (f. 25v).

Nineteen of the remaining twenty libraries sent out in these four years differed from the Oldbury library only in the contents of the second shelf, which held sixteen instead of twenty-one volumes. Instead of nos. 16–32 on this shelf (from Scott's Christian Life to King's Inventions of Men), costing £3 2s., these libraries had the following twelve volumes, costing £4 2s. 6d.

		£	s	d
16	Bp. Patrick's Commentary upon Genesis	8		
17	Exodus	8		
18	Leviticus	8		
19	Numbers	8		
20	Deuteronomy	8		
21	Ditto on Joshua, Judges and Ruth	8		
22	Ditto on the 2 Books of Samuel	8		
23	Ditto on the 2 Books of Kings	8		
24	Ditto on the Books of Chron : Ezra, Nehem' and Esther	8		
25	Bellarmine's Notes of the Church Examined etc.	7		
26	Camfield of Angels and Their Ministeries	2		
27	Bp. Beveridge's Explanation of the Church Catechism	1	6	

This selection of books was sent to the incumbents at Alnwick, Bampton, Burgh-by-Sands, Corston, *Darowen,* Dorchester, Evesham, Henley-in-Arden, Harrowden Parva, Kirkoswald, North Walsham, *Preston-by-Wingham,* Pwllheli, St. Bees, Sudbury, Tadcaster, Wentworth, Weobley, and Wigton.[2] Basically the same selection went to Alcester but with additions which raised the total number of volumes to seventy-four and the price to £29 16s. 6d.

Ten libraries were founded in the years 1720–7, at Llantysilio, *Poulton-le-Fylde,* Shepshed, Skelton (near Guisborough), Stowey, and Whitchurch (Hants) in 1720; at Malton and St. Martin's in 1721; at *Flookburgh* in 1725; at Shustoke in 1727.[2] The contents of only two of them are known from catalogues. The catalogue of the eighty-one volumes sent to Whitchurch is here printed in an abbreviated form from the printed sheet in Bodleian MS. Rawlinson D. 834, f. 31. The Malton catalogue, also on a printed sheet, is identical with it.[3] To judge from the extant books, the collection at Poulton-le-Fylde was the same and the collection at Flookburgh nearly the same as that at Whitchurch.[4] Titles which do not occur in the Oldbury catalogue are printed in full. For other titles the reader is referred to the Oldbury catalogue (above pp. 35–7).

[2] Italics show the surviving libraries.
[3] MS. Rawlinson D. 834, f. 34.   [4] See pp. 79 and 104.

A CATALOGUE of the Parochial Library at WHITCHURCH in Hampshire

SHELF I.					
	1	Eusebius. *Oldbury*, no. 1	1	1	6d
	2–4	Archbp. Tillotson's Works, 3 Vol. in Folio	2	8	
	5, 6	Whitby. *Oldbury*, nos. 3, 4	2	2	
	7	Pearson. *Oldbury*, no. 8		10	6
	8	Bray and Allen. *Oldbury*, no. 6		10	0
	9	Allen and Kettlewell. *Oldbury*, no. 7		8	
	10	Dr. More's Collection of Philosophical Writings		9	
	11	More. *Oldbury*, no. 10		16	
	12	The Register. *Oldbury*, no. 9		4	
			8	9	

SHELF II.					
	13	Bp. Bradford's Sermons at Mr. Boyle's Lectures		5	
	14	Mason's Sermon concerning the Authority of the Church in making Canons, etc.			8
	15–22	Bp. Blackall's Practical Discourses upon our Saviour's Sermon on the Mount, 8 Vol.	1	14	
	23	Comber. *Oldbury*, no. 56		5	
	24–5	Jenkins. *Oldbury*, nos. 52–3		9	
	26	Nelson's Address to Persons of Quality		3	6
	27	Nelson. *Oldbury*, no. 54		5	
	28–31	Lucas's Sermons, 4 Vol.		17	
	32	Kettlewell. *Oldbury*, no. 48		5	
	33	Kettlewell. *Oldbury*, no. 47		3	6
	34	Placette and Godeau. *Oldbury*, no. 15		5	
			4	12	8

SHELF III.					
	35–8	Abp. Sharp's Sermons, 4 Vols.	1		
	39–40	Arndtius de Vero Christianismo, 2 Vol.		11	
	41–2	Reeve. *Oldbury*, nos. 12, 13		9	
	43	Bennet. *Oldbury*, no. 60		3	6
	44	Bennet. *Oldbury*, no. 59		3	6
	45	Bennet. *Oldbury*, no. 58		3	6
	46	Ostervald. *Oldbury*, no. 21		4	
	47	Ostervald. *Oldbury*, no. 22		3	6
	48	Dunster's Drexelius on Eternity		3	6
	49	Howell. *Oldbury*, no. 25		3	6
	50	Bp. Smalridge's Sermons		5	
	51	Dr. Isham's Divine Philosophy		3	
	52	Goodman. *Oldbury*, no. 27		4	

	53	Wilkins. *Oldbury*, no. 61	4	
	54	Cave. *Oldbury*, no. 62	5	
	55	Spinckes. *Oldbury*, no. 64 (ii)	1	6
	56	Worthington. *Oldbury*, no. 64 (i)	3	

4 10 6

SHELF IV.	57	Abp. Wake's Sermons		4	6
	58	Dr. More's Divine Dialogues		4	
	59	—— Life		3	6
	60	—— Enchiridion Ethicum		2	6
	61	⎰ Mr. Le Fevre's Sufferings on Board the Galleys in France, and his Death in a Dungeon		1	6
		⎱ An Apologetical Vindication of the Church of England. *Oldbury*, no. 63 (i)		1	6
	62	Bonnell. *Oldbury*, no. 65		3	0
	63	Bp. Burnett's Pastoral Care		2	6
		Goodman. *Oldbury*, no. 28		3	
	64	Mocket's Politia Ecclesiae Anglicanae		1	
		⎰ Zouch's Descriptio Juris et Judicii Ecclesiast. secund. Can. Anglic.			9
		⎱ —— Descriptio Juris et Judicii Temporalis secundum Consuetudines Feudales et Normanicas			9
	65	March's Sermons		3	
	66	Nelson's Practice of True Devotion		2	6
	67–70	Dupin's Church History abridg'd, 4 Vol.		10	
	71	Allen. *Oldbury*, no. 70 (i)		1	6
	72	Lucas. *Oldbury*, no. 31		2	6
	73	Clarke. *Oldbury*, no. 68 (i)		1	6
	74	Wall. *Oldbury*, no. 68 (ii)			4
	75	King. *Oldbury*, no. 32		1	6
	76	Kettlewell. *Oldbury*, no. 71		1	6
	77	Addison's Christian's Daily Sacrifice		1	0
	78	Gastrell. *Oldbury*, no. 50		2	6
	79	Bray. *Oldbury*, no. 66		4	
	80	⎰ Bp. Beveridge's Church Catechism explain'd			9
		⎱ Ostervald's Grounds and Principles of the Christian Religion explain'd		2	
	81	Beveridge. *Oldbury*, no. 51		3	

3 6 1

Brought from the	I. Shelf	8	9	
	II. Shelf	4	12	8
	III. Shelf	4	10	6
	IV. Shelf	3	6	1
The Case		1	6	
Packing, Carriage, etc. of incidental Charges		1	5	
		23	9	3

D. *Book-cupboards*. Each library sent out in 1710–13 was packed in a wainscot cupboard of 'best Season'd Oak' (Minutes, 1708, p. 37) costing 25s. The cupboards had handles for easy transport and contained four shelves. The bottom shelf was made tall enough to take Henry More's Works, a fairly large folio. The other shelves were for small books. The cupboard in the church at Preston-by-Wingham still contains its books. At Bridlington books and cupboard [5] are kept separately. Cupboards without books are at Llanrhos in the church and at Flaxley in the rectory. The upper half of the cupboard remains in All Saints' Church, Evesham. A catalogue of the books and a copy of the Act of 7 Anne were pasted inside the door of each cupboard. The number 32 painted on the outside of the door of the cupboard at Evesham is the number assigned to the library sent to Evesham. The library sent to Flookburgh in 1725 was in '2 cases cover'd with Matts.' [6]

E. *Bonds*. The Rules of Parochial Libraries and the form of words whereby the recipients of a library promised to observe the Rules under pain of a penalty of £30 [7] were printed on a pair of leaves and sent to incumbents, who signed them in the presence of witnesses and returned them to Newman. Copies of these bonds signed by the incumbents of Alcester, Llanrhos, Malton, Poulton, Shepshed, and Whitchurch are in the Bodleian Library, MS. Rawlinson D. 834, ff. 18, 23, 34, 28, 26, 32.

[5] See pl. I (*a*).
[6] See p. 31.
[7] See p. 32.

F

III. DATES OF FOUNDATION OF LIBRARIES

1573	*Guildford* (see p. 16) [1]
By 1586–7	Leicester
1595	Bury St. Edmunds
By 1597 (?)	Newcastle
1598	Grantham
1599	Ipswich
By 1606	Ecclesfield
1608	*Norwich* (see p. 16) [1]
1613	*Bristol* (see p. 16) [1]
1615	Tankersley
1616	Oakham
1617	King's Lynn (S. Nicholas)
1619	Totnes
c. 1619	Bath
1622 (?)	Swaffham
1624–8	Halifax
Before 1626	Stamford
By 1629	Norwich (S. Peter Mancroft)
1631	King's Lynn (S. Margaret)
	Langley Marish
1632	*Colchester* (see p. 17) [1]
1634	Boston
Before 1636	Bury (Lancashire)
1637	Spalding
c. 1640	Manchester
1646	Southampton
By 1652	Wootton Wawen
1653	Bolton
	Gorton
	Turton
c. 1660	Wisbech
1661	Birmingham (S. Martin)
By 1661	Shiplake
By 1662	King's Norton
1664	Barnstaple
c. 1665	Hull (Holy Trinity)

[1] The dates of foundation of some libraries not included in the alphabetical list but referred to in the Introduction or in the *Life and Designs of Thomas Bray*, ed. 1808, pp. 81–2, have been included. These entries are in italics.

By 1672	Ottery St. Mary
1677	Chirbury
1678	Marlborough
1679	Chelmsford
1680	Milton Abbas
	More
By 1682	Hull (S. Mary Lowgate)
1684	London (S. Martin-in-the-Fields)
	Ribchester
1685	North Grimston
	Wimborne
	Ten libraries of B. Oley's foundation (see pp. 18–19)
1690	Assington
	Salford
By 1691	Bicester
1693	Denchworth
1694	Stainton
1695	Cudworth
	Martock
	Willen
1697	Cartmel
	Tong
1698	Newark
1699	Beverley (S. Mary)
	Coniston
1700	Bedford
	Hackness
c. 1700	Beccles
1701	Costock
	Durham (S. Oswald)
	Reigate
	Warwick (S. Mary)
By 1701	Northampton
1703	Bilston
	Milden
	Sleaford
By 1703	Basingstoke
1704	Lawshall
	Maldon
	Rotherham
c. 1704	Nantwich
By 1705	Sheldon
	Womersley

43

c. 1705	Sheffield
	Southwell (see p. 22) [2]
	York (S. Mary Castlegate)
By 1707	Barton-on-Humber
1708	Hatfield Broad Oak
By 1708	Skipton
1710	Wotton-under-Edge
	Twenty-two S.P.C.K. libraries (see p. 23)
1711	Fifteen S.P.C.K. libraries (see p. 23)
1712	Earl Sterndale
	Wisbech revived
	Fourteen S.P.C.K. libraries (see p. 23)
1713	Oldbury
1714	Ashby-de-la-Zouch
	Doncaster
	King's Lynn augmented
	Rougham
1715	Hereford (All Saints)
	Liverpool
	Tiverton
1715 (?)	Brent Eleigh
By 1715	Cranfield
By 1716	Maidstone
	Withington
1717	Bassingbourne
	Whitchurch (Shropshire)
1718	Gillingham
1719	Boston augmented
	Stoke-by-Nayland
1720	Bradfield
	Lewes
	Six S.P.C.K. libraries (see p. 24)
1721	Crediton
	Hillingdon
	Two S.P.C.K. libraries (see p. 24)
1723 (?)	Kildwick
1724	Basingstoke augmented
	Effingham
	Slaithwaite
1725	East Harlsey
	Flookburgh

[2] The dates of foundation of some libraries not included in the alphabetical list but referred to in the Introduction or in the *Life and Designs of Thomas Bray*, ed. 1808, pp. 81–2, have been included. These entries are in italics.

1727	Ashby-de-la-Zouch augmented
	Shustoke
By 1727	Woodchurch
1728	Crundale
1729	Corbridge
1730	Coleshill
	Ledsham
	London (S. Botolph, Aldgate)
	Sheldon augmented
1730 (?)	Amberley
c. 1730	*How* (see p. 24) [3]
	Streatley (see p. 24) [3]
1731	Newport Pagnell
	Whitchurch (Hampshire) augmented
1732	Elston
1733	Birmingham (S. Philip)
	Bishop's Lydeard
	Halton
	Sible Hedingham
1734	Astley
	Willen augmented
1735	Maidstone augmented
	Newcastle-on-Tyne augmented
1737	Henley-on-Thames
	Newent
1737 (?)	Broughton
1740	Bromham
	Heathfield
1741	Swinderby
1743	Bridgnorth
	Doddington
	Mentmore
1745	Newcastle augmented
	Tong augmented
1747	Lanteglos-by-Camelford
By 1747	Bubwith
1749	Bratton Fleming
	Norton (Derbyshire)
By 1750	Chippenham
1751	Bampton augmented
By 1751	Thurnham

[3] The dates of foundation of some libraries not included in the alphabetical list but referred to in the Introduction or in the *Life and Designs of Thomas Bray,* ed. 1808, pp. 81–2, have been included. These entries are in italics.

1752	King's Cliffe
1755	Stanground
1757	Tortworth
	Eighteen libraries of the Associates of Dr. Bray [4]
1760	*Ford* [4]
1761	*Fifteen libraries of the Associates of Dr. Bray* [4]
1763	London (S. Leonard Shoreditch)
1763	Stonehouse
1764	*Llanwnog* [4]
	Wendlebury
1764 (?)	Shipdham
1765	Grantham augmented
	Offord Cluny
	Westerham
	Fourteen libraries of the Associates of Dr. Bray [4]
1766	Graveley
	Fifteen libraries of the Associates of Dr. Bray [4]
1768	*Eight libraries of the Associates of Dr. Bray* [4]
1768 (?)	Royston
1777	Northampton augmented
1783	St. Neots augmented
1784	Norton-cum-Lenchwick
1785	Loughborough
By 1785	Woodbridge
1788	Finedon
	Wentnor
1795	Beetham
1796	Plymtree
1809	Elham
1819	Bewdley
	Castleton
1828	Steeple Ashton
	Myddle (see p. 24) [4]
	Whitchurch (Salop) augmented

[4] The dates of foundation of some libraries not included in the alphabetical list but referred to in the Introduction or in the *Life and Designs of Thomas Bray,* ed. 1808, pp. 81–2, have been included. These entries are in italics.

1841	Oxford (S. Peter-in-the-East)
1849	Yelden
1862	Halifax augmented
1869	Donington
1883	Prees
1890	*Eastbourne (All Saints)* (see p. 24)[5]

---

[5] The dates of foundation of some libraries not included in the alphabetical list but referred to in the Introduction or in the *Life and Designs of Thomas Bray,* ed. 1808, pp. 81–2, have been included. These entries are in italics.

THE ACT OF 7 ANNE C. 14 RELATING TO PAROCHIAL LIBRARIES

C A P. XIV.

An Act for the better Preservation of Parochial Libraries in that Part o
Great Britain called *England.*

'W H E R E A S in many Places in the South Parts of *Great Britain* called *Englan*
'and *Wales,* the Provision for the Clergy is so mean, that the necessary Expenc
'of Books for the better Prosecution of their Studies cannot be defrayed b
'them ; and whereas of late Years, several charitable and well-disposed Person
'have by charitable Contributions erected Libraries within several Parishes an
'Districts in *England,* and *Wales* ; but some Provision is wanting to preserve th
'same, and such others as shall be provided in the same Manner, from Em
'bezilment ;' Be it therefore enacted by the Queen's most Excellent Majesty, b
and with the Advice and Consent of the Lords Spiritual and Temporal, an
Commons, in this present Parliament assembled, and by the Authority of th
same, That in every Parish or Place where such a Library is or shall be erected
the same shall be preserved for such Use and Uses, as the same is and shall b
given, and the Orders and Rules of the Founder and Founders of such Librarie
shall be observed and kept.

II. And for the Encouragement of such Founders and Benefactors, and t
the Intent they may be satisfied, that their pious and charitable Intent may n
be frustrated ; Be it also enacted by the Authority aforesaid, That every Incum
bent, Rector, Vicar, Minister or Curate of a Parish, before he shall be per
mitted to use and enjoy such Library, shall enter into such Security by Bond o
otherwise, for Preservation of such Library, and due Observance of the Rule
and Orders belonging to the same, as the proper Ordinaries within their respec
tive Jurisdictions, in their Discretion shall think fit ; and in case any Book o
Books belonging to the said Library shall be taken away and detained, it sha
and may be lawful for the said Incumbent, Rector, Vicar, Minister or Curat
for the Time being, or any other Person or Persons, to bring an Action o
Trover and Conversion, in the Name of the proper Ordinaries within thei
respective Jurisdictions ; whereupon Treble Damages shall be given with fu
Costs of Suit, as if the same were his or their proper Book or Books, whic
Damages shall be applied to the Use and Benefit of the said Library.

III. And it is further enacted by the Authority aforesaid, That it shall an
may be lawful to and for the proper Ordinary, or his Commissary or Offici
in his respective Jurisdiction, or the Archdeacon, or by his Direction his Offici
or Surrogate, if the said Archdeacon be not the Incumbent of the Place wher
such Library is, in his or their respective Visitation, to enquire into the Stat
and Condition of the said Libraries, and to amend and redress the Grievanc
and Defects of and concerning the same, as to him or them shall seem meet
and it shall and may be lawful to and for the proper Ordinary, from time t
time, as often as shall be thought fit, to appoint such Person or Persons, as h

Side notes:

In every Parish where a Library shall be erected, it shall be preserved for the Uses to which it is given, &c.

Incumbents, &c. before they use the Library, shall give Security to preserve it.

If any Book be taken away &c. the Incumbent may bring Trover, and shall recover Treble Damages, to the Use of the Library.

The Ordinary, &c. may inquire into the State of the Library, and amend the Defects ; and appoint Persons to inspect the Library.

48

NOTES ON EARLY PRINTED BOOKS AND THEIR CARE

PRINTING was invented half-way through the fifteenth century, probably by Johann Gutenberg of Mainz, and came to this country via the Low Countries where Caxton was originally a merchant. In Germany, the Low Countries and England, the 'black letter' type, based on the Gothic handwriting in use in the fifteenth century, was at first the rule; it is the ancestor of the modern German printing type. In Italy, however, there had been a widespread adoption, by a series of scholar printers, of the roman and italic forms of handwriting as a basis for printing types; these gradually spread northward and ousted the 'black letter' types.

Books of this period, from the middle of the fifteenth century to 1501, are known as incunabula. The known copies of them have been carefully recorded by librarians in works of reference, such as R. G. C. Proctor, *An Index to the Early Printed Books in the British Museum from the Invention of Printing to the year MD. With Notes of those in the Bodleian Library*, 1898–9, and J. C. T. Oates, *Catalogue of the fifteenth century Printed Books in the University Library, Cambridge*, 1954.

To the sixteenth century belong the various Bibles, such as the Bishop's Bible, and the First and Second Prayer Books of Edward VI. Original editions of these are not common, and are of considerable interest. Books of this period are often in the type to which we have become accustomed, but the 'black letter' still continued to be used.

Both incunabula and books printed in the first two or three decades of the sixteenth century are worth special care, and if they have not already been recorded in a printed catalogue, their existence should be reported to the Diocesan Advisory Committee.

The bulk of the books in a parochial library is likely to belong to the seventeenth and eighteenth centuries—volumes of sermons and controversy excellently printed in roman type on rag-paper and bound in calf. They are less rare, but are nevertheless of interest and importance as illustrating the kind of question which exercised the minds of our forefathers.

For those who are tempted to study further the fascinating history of early printing, an introduction is supplied by Francis Meynell in his *English printed books*, 1946, in Collins' *'Britain in Pictures'* series. More detailed books are—N. E. Binns, *An Introduction to Historical Bibliography*, 1953; R. B. McKerrow, *An Introduction to Bibliography for*

Literary Students, 2nd impr., 1928; E. Gordon Duff, *Early Printed Books* (Books about Books), 1893; A. J. K. Esdaile, *A Student's Manual of Bibliography,* 3rd ed., 1954; Alfred W. Pollard, *Early Illustrated Books* (Books about Books), 1893. Duff's and Pollard's books are out of print, but are generally available through urban public or county libraries.

Arrangement of Books

If the original shelving, book-desks or bookcases remain, these should continue to be used. On no account should ancient furniture be altered to suit modern needs, as was done recently in a Midland parish where a glass front was fitted to a unique seventeenth-century book-desk.

It may be that the shelves have a 'press-mark,' that is a number or a letter, or both. If this is so, and if the books are also marked with press-marks, the question of arrangement has been solved for us.

Where modern shelving is used, books should be sorted into subjects so far as possible, and sets of volumes kept together. It will often be found convenient to arrange books in sequences according to size—folio, quarto and octavo—but keeping them grouped in subjects in each sequence. Otherwise smaller books may tend to be pushed to the back and lost.

List of Contents

Every parochial library should be checked from time to time against a list of its contents to make sure that nothing is missing. It will be remembered that it was as a result of such a checking that the famous copy of Caxton's *Legenda secundum usum Sarum* was found in the parochial library of S. Mary's, Warwick. This book was in the library in 1709, the date of the earliest surviving catalogue, but it seems to have escaped notice when the library was again catalogued in 1880. Had the forefathers of the present parishioners been a little more careful over checking, this treasure would not have been lost to view for so long.

The form which the list should take will vary with local circumstances. For simple checking purposes, a list of the books, shelf by shelf, under the authors' names, will suffice, but for a more elaborate catalogue— and the committee hope that these will generally be made eventually— incumbents should seek professional advice and help. One of the people suggested in the Report on p. 61 should be consulted.

Care of bindings

The bindings of books in parochial libraries are often dilapidated, but this does not mean that they are unworthy or incapable of preservation. Leather bindings of all kinds should be 'oiled' from time to time: a useful dressing, employed by the British Museum Library, consists of: —

Lanolin (anhydrous)	7 oz. (avoir.)
Cedarwood oil	1 oz. (fluid)
Beeswax	$\frac{1}{2}$ oz. (avoir.)
Hexane (or petroleum ether B.P. 60°–80° C.)	11 oz. (fluid)

The mixture, which is obtainable through branches of Boots (Cash Chemists) Ltd., is a lanolin lubricant to which has been added enough wax to consolidate superficial powdery decay. Take each calf-bound book, brush off the dust with a soft brush, paste down any torn corners etc. of the leather. Apply the dressing, well-shaken, liberally to the back and joints, with 'mutton cloth,' more sparingly to the dies, rubbing it into the leather. Allow the volumes to remain on a table for twenty-four hours, and give them a rub with a cloth, before replacing them on the shelves: they will still be found to be a little 'tacky,' but so long as they are not too tight on the shelves they will not stick to each other. The 'tackiness' will disappear in a few weeks after which the leather will merely feel pleasantly supple.

The mixture is highly inflammable and no naked light must be allowed in the room during application and for some time afterwards. It is advisable to acquire it in fairly small quantities.

White vellum books can be carefully washed with a slightly damp sponge and a little 'Propert's' saddle soap. Concentrate on the backs of the bindings. When vellum books are dry, they can be treated very sparingly with the British Museum dressing and the bindings polished after a few hours.

Repairs to bindings should be attempted with very great caution, as incompetent work with paper, paste and tape may lessen the value of the book, and it is unlikely to be permanent. Those who wish to make a thorough study of the question of bindings and their repair are recommended to read *Bookbinding and the Care of Books* by Douglas Cockerell, 4th ed., 1945, and *The Preservation of Leather Bookbinding* by H. J. Plenderleith, 1953.

In some areas the local education authority may be willing to organize classes in book-binding if enough students are forthcoming.

The study of bindings is of great interest both from the artistic aspect, and from the point of view of the type of materials used. It comes as a surprise to many people to discover that the covers of old books are often of wood—a material which presents its own problems, since it may become a hunting ground for insect pests, a subject to be dealt with later.

During the seventeenth and eighteenth centuries the cheaper type of book was bound in sheepskin, whilst the more valuable were bound in calf or morocco. The calfskin of this period lasts well, but nineteenth century calfskin is less durable because it was tanned by a different process.

Those who wish to know more of the history of binding should read J. B. Oldham, *English Blind Stamped Bindings,* 1952.

If a book seems to be worthy of expert repair, a professional librarian should be consulted. Some large public and university libraries have their own bindery which may be able to help; otherwise a professional librarian will be able to recommend a firm or individual accustomed to deal with the repair and rebinding of old books by hand. Many otherwise admirable firms have no one on their staff capable of undertaking work of this sort. Machine binding is a comparatively recent development, dating only from the latter part of the nineteenth century. Contemporary bindings, especially those bearing decoration, should wherever possible be repaired conservatively, and not rebound. Books are like old buildings in this respect.

Especial care should be taken of end-papers (the paper used in binding), and any loose notes found in books. The end-papers may include a 'cancel,' that is, a page rejected, for some reason, by the printer, which may add considerably to the interest of the book. Fragments of medieval manuscripts, especially service books, are often found inside bindings of the seventeenth century and earlier. Loose papers and book-marks may be removed, but it is important that anything taken out of a book should be scrutinized before being thrown away. One such small folded paper proved to be a note written in 1637 to tell a doctor that an old patient of his required 'another box of the same pills.' Another, apparently of the late eighteenth century read: 'Reverend Sir, Please to give us poor Blue boys a holiday for to go and see the Volunteers.' Such small and homely instances give point to the Public Record Office's insistence on the historical importance of documentary evidence of all sorts, and we must learn to appreciate the value to historians even of old bills and letters which have been long forgotten.

Chains, and clasps too, form part of the original history of the book, and should not be lightly discarded. They should occasionally be slightly oiled to keep them free from rust.

The enemies of books

The principal enemies of books are damp, strong heat and light, and various insect pests.

54

Paper, like most other substances, contains a certain amount of natural moisture. If books are packed tightly on the shelves, or kept perpetually locked in a safe or strong room, or even in a cupboard with a wooden or glass door which is always kept closed so that air cannot circulate freely among them, the amount of moisture may become excessive, because there is no opportunity for the natural process of evaporation. Excessive moisture may lead to decay of paper and the growth of fungi.

Strong light and heat, on the other hand, may cause the natural moisture in the paper and leather to dry up, with the result that the pages become wavy at the edges and the bindings, buckled.

Possibly the worst insect likely to attack books is the Brown House or False Clothes Moth: the caterpillar attacks bindings, both leather and cloth; it may bore through the pages and often makes holes in the hinge where the boards join the back. The common Clothes Moth can also attack bindings. The common Furniture Beetle damages books, but usually when the adult is trying to emerge from woodwork and finds a book in the way. Certain spider beetles will attack bindings and paper; they leave a lace-like pattern of destruction and fretted edges to the pages; in general they do not, however, do extensive damage to books in this country. Both the common and German Cockroaches can damage bindings and papers; bindings often have a blotchy appearance as a result of their activities.

The best method of preventing damage by both damp and insect pests is to allow air to circulate freely among the books, and to move them about from time to time. Do not pack them too tightly on the shelves, and remember that if they are to be kept in a modern locked cupboard, a grille is better than a glass door. Books kept in a safe should be taken out for an airing from time to time, and it is a good plan for any one who is going to be present in the vestry, or other room where the safe is, for some little time, to keep the door of the safe open whilst he is there.

Experience has shown that books which are frequently moved about are seldom attacked by insect pests, and by taking these simple precautions, much damage can be avoided, but should it be found that books are damaged as the result of active infestation, they can be fumigated by being placed in strong paper or plastic bags or tin boxes, with paradichlorobenzene crystals, at a concentration of $\frac{1}{2}$ lb. to 5 cubic feet of air. These containers, sealed with gummed tape, should be left for a fortnight in a warm room before being opened.

REPORT OF THE PAROCHIAL LIBRARIES COMMITTEE OF THE CENTRAL COUNCIL FOR THE CARE OF CHURCHES

IN 1949 the Archbishop of Canterbury asked the Central Council for the Care of Churches to make a report on the number and condition of parochial libraries still in existence, and to add recommendations for their future preservation.

The following members of the Committee were appointed in November 1949:—

The Archdeacon of Wisbech, the Ven. S. J. A. Evans, M.A., F.S.A. (Chairman)[1]

Dr. F. C. Eeles, O.B.E., LL.D., LITT.D., F.S.A. (SCOT).[2]

Mr. F. C. Francis, M.A., F.S.A.

Miss M. S. G. Hands[3]

Mr. Raymond Richards, M.A., F.S.A.

Mr. Lawrence Tanner, C.V.O., M.A., F.S.A.

Mr. F. C. Morgan, M.A., F.S.A., F.L.A. (Hon. Secretary).

Mr. W. A. Munford, M.B.E., B.SC. (ECON.), F.L.A., now Director-General of the National Library for the Blind, was appointed in June 1950 by the Library Association, to represent them, and Mr. Neil Ker, B.LITT., M.A., Reader in Palaeography in the University of Oxford and Fellow of Magdalen College, was co-opted in November 1957. The Committee were gratified that Her Majesty the Queen bestowed the order of Companion of the Bath upon one of their number, Mr. F. C. Francis, in 1958.

The Committee has held ten meetings. Its recommendations are appended to this report.

In order to make both the alphabetical list of remaining libraries and these recommendations more useful and more intelligible the Committee has added an historical introduction to the subject, together with practical hints on the care of books.

The Committee was mainly concerned with those collections which, it feels, can properly be called parochial libraries, that is to say, collections of a dozen or more books belonging to the church and formed for the benefit of clergy or parishioners or both, but it does not wish to

[1] Since 1953, Dean of Gloucester.
[2] Dr. Eeles died in August 1954.
[3] Since March 1956, Mrs. Neil MacLeod.

56

exclude from its Report and Recommendations the Bibles and Prayer Books of the eighteenth century and earlier, the medieval service books in print and manuscript, and the copies of such books as Erasmus's *Paraphrases* and Jewel's *Works* now existing in many churches where there is no library proper. These isolated books are sometimes important and sometimes of particular local interest. Many of them are, or have been, chained to a desk in the church, and figure in the lists compiled by William Blades and J. Charles Cox.[4]

A few libraries in churches are, it seems, not church property, and therefore not within the scope of this Report. These are included in the Alphabetical List which accompanies it. This list also includes some town libraries, which were probably originally in the church, but which are now housed elsewhere. Such collections have generally been taken over by the urban public or county libraries.

The Committee has made very thorough enquiries concerning parochial libraries, but it is conscious that these may well not be exhaustive. It would be grateful if information about material which has eluded it could be sent to the Librarian, Central Council for the Care of Churches, Fulham Palace, London, S.W. 6.

Since the Committee began to hold its meetings, certain events have come to its notice which only serve to show the need to impress upon clergy and laity alike the importance of taking proper care of these libraries. The witness of the Church of England is perhaps weakest to-day in learned, literary and artistic circles, and the failure to safeguard our bibliographical treasures is hardly likely to strengthen it. Since the first world war, these libraries have been menaced by a new enemy in addition to the attacks of damp, neglect and vandalism, from which they have suffered ever since the eighteenth century. This is the urgent need for ready cash which hampers all who have the care of our parish churches. Again and again, and still to-day, the clergy and their parishioners, in need of money for church repair, have turned to their parochial libraries as an asset that can sometimes be raided to help them out of a tight financial corner. It is the opinion of the Committee that this ought to be prevented. Most of these libraries are perpetual bequests to the clergy or to their parishioners, and it is submitted that the present generation ought not to dissipate church property which has been handed down from the past in order to finance some present need. The Committee would also like to emphasize that a parochial library is a 'monument'; and just as people are learning to value the rich heritage of funerary

---

[4] William Blades, *Books in Chains,* 1892. J. Charles Cox, *English Church Furniture,* Antiquary's Books, Methuen, 1907, pp. 337–40.

H

sculpture in which our parish churches abound, so they must come to recognize the parochial library as having an identity of its own. A picture of the traditions and learnings of another age would be lost if the collection were to be dispersed.

In the past few years there have been at least six sales of books or of whole libraries. Shortly after its meetings began, the Committee was shocked to learn that the famous Shipdham Parochial Library had been offered for sale in London under a faculty of the Consistory Court of Norwich without any consultation with the Diocesan Advisory Committee. As the faculty was some years old, the present Chancellor advised postponement of the sale, in order that the protests of the Central Council for the Care of Churches, and of others, might be considered. Nevertheless, in spite of these, and of the wish expressed by the Archbishop of Canterbury in a letter to the Chairman that any steps taken, as at Shipdham, to sell church books should be postponed until the report of this Committee had been presented to him, the sale of most of the library eventually took place in March 1951. The remainder of the books are now accommodated at the Norwich City Library and are called the Shipdham Parochial Library.

Other cases of sales were those of Norton-cum-Lenchwick, in Worcestershire, where a collection of about 360 volumes was sold without authority in 1951, a particularly bad instance. At Flaxley, in Gloucestershire, books are believed to have been sold, also without authority, with the goods of a deceased incumbent in 1948.

As already stated, the fact that books have been given or left to a parish in perpetuity does not appear to act as a deterrent to sales. Although William Whitehead, rector of Stanground, Huntingdonshire, bequeathed his library *'in usum successorum,'* appointing the rectors of Woodston and Fletton as trustees, *'ut integra semper descendat,'* his successor in 1950 informed the Central Council that he had sold the library a few years before for £90, 'after permission from all concerned.'

The most recent sale [4a] of a complete parochial library which has come to the Committee's notice is that of the collection of books at Royston, Herts, in 1953. A collection of thirty old books, found during the restoration of the tower roof, was sold to a parishioner for £10, without a faculty being applied for, and another thirty-nine books were apparently sold to a Cambridge bookseller. This library was not included in the inventory of church goods.

Two deplorable cases of wanton and deliberate destruction by incumbents have also been noted. The first of these occurred at Hillingdon,

[4a] Since this Report went to press, a faculty was granted by the Chancellor of the Diocese of Ely, after consultation with the Diocesan Advisory Committee, for the sale of Broughton Parochial Library to Cambridge University Library.

Middlesex, where, according to information received by the Central Council in 1950, a large and once valuable library was burned, except for a copy of *Eikon Basilike* which was rescued by the verger. Fuller particulars of the contents of this library may be found in the Alphabetical List.

Another reprehensible case is that of Coniston, Lancs, where a small collection of books was thrown away in 1957, on the grounds that it was dusty and untidy, and hindered the labours of those responsible for cleaning the church. This also involved a breach of faith with a past benefactor, who had left an annual endowment of 8s. 4d. for the upkeep of the parochial library.

The Committee note that valuable furniture in parochial libraries has not always been treated with respect. At Wootton Wawen, Warwickshire, the seventeenth-century book-desk for chained books, which is of great interest, and probably unique,[5] has been converted into a show case in a misguided attempt to preserve the books from damage.

The rediscovery of a unique Caxton in the parochial library of S. Mary's, Warwick, by a member of the staff of the Birmingham University Library, serves to underline the need for the cataloguing of these libraries by professional librarians, and for the careful checking of their contents against the catalogue at regular intervals. This book was included in the earliest surviving catalogue of the library, made in 1709, but was apparently lost to view when the library was recatalogued in 1880. A faculty has recently been granted by the Consistory Court of the Diocese of Coventry, permitting the sale of this book to the British Museum. The Committee whilst appreciating the difficulties in which the parish finds itself, and realizing that the book will now be more easily accessible to scholars, deplores its alienation.

The Committee is pleased to note signs of reviving interest in these libraries, and hope that the publication of this report will stimulate incumbents and parishioners to take more care of them in the future, and perhaps to repurchase books when occasion offers. Professional advice on both cataloguing and repairs will be available generally from the urban public or county librarian, and these officials and their staffs will usually be found to take an interest in the parochial library. A letter from the office of the Central Council for the Care of Churches, urging them to offer their assistance, appeared in the *Library Association Record* for January 1957.

Should a parish be in a position of special difficulty over paying for repairs to books in a parochial library, application should be made to the Librarian, Central Council for the Care of Churches, Fulham

---

[5] Pl. IV (c). B. H. Streeter, *The Chained Library*, 1931, pp. 24, 290, 292.

Palace, London, S.W. 6, as it is possible that a small grant from a charitable fund which it administers might be forthcoming.

The Committee feels it a matter for great regret that the Act of March 1708–9 (7 Anne c. 14) 'for the better Preservation of Parochial Libraries in that Part of Great Britain called England,' which is still on the Statute Book, should so seldom be invoked for their protection. The Act should afford protection to all parochial libraries established after 1708. Further notes on its scope, with the excellent provisions it makes for regular checking of books and certification of the inventory, are given on p. 21 of the historical introduction to this report.

It is sufficient here to cite Section X.

> 'And it is further enacted and declared by the Authority aforesaid, That none of the said Books shall in any Case be alienable, nor any Book or Books that shall hereafter be given by any Benefactor or Benefactors shall be alienated, without the Consent of the proper Ordinary, and then only when there is a Duplicate of such Book or Books; and that in case any Book or Books be taken or otherwise lost out of the said Library, it shall and may be lawful to and for any Justice of Peace within the County, Riding, or Division, to grant his Warrant to search for the same, and in case the same be found, such Book or Books so found shall immediately, by Order of such Justice, be restored to the said Library; any Law, Statute, or Usage to the contrary in any wise notwithstanding.'

The only exemption from the provisions of this Act is afforded by Section 4 of the Faculty Jurisdiction Measure, 1938, which states that: —

> '(1) Notwithstanding anything to the contrary contained in section ten of the Parochial Libraries Act, 1708, any book in a parochial library appropriated to the use of the minister of any parish or place within the operation of that Act may be sold under the authority of a faculty issuing out of the consistory court of the diocese in which the parish concerned is situate, and in the case of every sale so authorised the proceeds of sale shall be applied for such of the ecclesiastical purposes of the parish as in such faculty may be directed.
>
> '(2) Any question whether a library is within the said Act and is so appropriated shall be finally determined by the Charity Commissioners.'

It would appear that this would enable a parochial library to be sold with the permission of the Consistory Court, but as has been stated in the recommendations appended to this report, the Committee generally strongly deprecates such sales, and must trust that in future, in all cases where such a sale is contemplated, the Diocesan Advisory Committee will be consulted by the Chancellor before reaching a decision.

Signed. SEIRIOL J. A. EVANS,
Chairman, Central Council for
the Care of Churches.

The Deanery, Gloucester.

Signed. F. C. MORGAN,
Secretary of the Committee.

Hereford.

RECOMMENDATIONS OF THE COMMITTEE

THE historical introduction to our report and the extensive schedule of parochial libraries, large and small, which accompanies it, indicate clearly enough that we have to deal with an interesting and valuable department of church property. We now offer the following recommendations for its maintenance and safety.

1. It is at present possible for a parochial library to be sold under faculty of the Consistory Court without the knowledge of the Diocesan Advisory Committee, or of the Archdeacon, or even of the Bishop of the diocese; on the mere application of the parochial authorities and the consent of the Chancellor, without wider consultation.

WE RECOMMEND therefore that the Diocesan Advisory Committee ought to be consulted in any application for a faculty for the sale of church books, and that the Faculty Jurisdiction Measure, 1938, Section 4, should be amended by adding a clause, (3) to the following effect:—

'(3) Any application for the sale of a parochial library or any church books shall be deemed to come within the purview of the Diocesan Advisory Committee, who shall be required to advise the petitioners and report to the Chancellor.'

2. We now turn to problems of maintenance.

WE RECOMMEND that unless circumstances absolutely forbid, a parochial library ought to be retained in its own home. We recognize that this ideal cannot always be upheld, and we offer below some suggestions for transference to other custody. We think, however, that much more can be done to maintain these libraries in the parish than is usually attempted.

(i) To this end, we think that the Diocesan Advisory Committee should have general supervision of parochial libraries, as they have of other church valuables. To assist them in their task we suggest that the Bishop should appoint an extra member or adviser who could be consulted on the care of church books. In many dioceses it would be possible to enlist the interest and assistance of professional librarians at an urban public, county or university library; and other professional assistance might be forthcoming from the county record office or museum staff. In this way it should be possible for every Diocesan Advisory Committee to have available some competent and enthusiastic bibliographer round whom the interest in parochial libraries might centre.

(ii) Every library should have an up-to-date catalogue. The preparation of a proper catalogue, in which the edition, the printer, and the peculiarities, if any, of the individual copy of each book, are correctly noted, requires expert advice. The qualified member of the Diocesan Advisory Committee should be able to provide this, or to indicate where it may be obtained. As a temporary expedient, a simple *list* might be made by the incumbent or local schoolmaster, a copy of which should be appended to the Inventory of Church Goods and Ornaments in the church safe.

(iii) Besides the expert at the centre, there should always be an amateur at the circumference, and we think that where there is a considerable library, it ought usually to be possible to find in the locality a voluntary custodian, who could be taught enough about the books by the expert to make the charge interesting. Such a person should, as his first and continuing task, check the shelves with the existing catalogue, if any.

3. WE RECOMMEND that when it appears that the existence of a library is endangered by its being allowed to remain in its place of origin, either because of unsuitable accommodation or lack of local interest, it should be reported on by an expert, and that the books should be offered to, or deposited on loan with, some library in the vicinity—e.g. the urban public or county library, a cathedral library, or a university library. In order to preserve the identity of the collection, the books might be kept together and marked, 'The . . . . . . Parochial Library.' Where this is done a formal receipt should be obtained in duplicate, and one copy deposited in the diocesan registry, the other in the church safe, and an entry made in the church inventory.

4. WE RECOMMEND as a final safeguard that additional questions about the parochial library, if any, should be added to the Form of the Inventory of Church Goods when this is revised. We suggest that incumbents should be asked to state whether the library contains any books printed before 1501, and whether there is a catalogue of the library.

5. Our investigation, from the nature of things, has been no more than a preliminary survey of the ground: what is now required is a more detailed combined descriptive catalogue of the libraries and of the books which they contain. It would be a task parallel to those recently undertaken by the generosity of the Pilgrim Trust in the cathedral libraries and in capitular and episcopal archives, and it would demand the services of a qualified investigator and appropriate funds. We consider this to be the most necessary step in any integrated plan for the preservation of these libraries.

ALPHABETICAL LIST OF PAROCHIAL LIBRARIES
PAST AND PRESENT

THE libraries listed (*a*) contain or are known to have contained, at least a dozen books printed before 1800, and (*b*) are, or were, kept in a church or parsonage or in a building close to a church. Five other libraries which are not strictly covered by this definition are also included, because they are, or apparently were, akin to parochial libraries. These are Halton (Cheshire), King's Cliffe and Maldon, which are housed in special library buildings, Lewes, which does not appear to have had a home, and Ludlow of which nothing is known apart from an inscription in two existing books which records that they belonged 'ad librariam ecclesie ludloiensis.' In all, 253 libraries are listed.

Some thirty-five libraries mentioned by Blades in his list of 'Minor libraries' in *The Bookworm* for 1866, pp. 135, 157–8, 172–3, have not been included in the list, because nothing has been discovered about them. Some of them no doubt existed, but some may have been listed by Blades in error, e.g. Bramham, Eltham, and Monk's Eleigh, for Bromham, Elham, and Brent Eleigh.

Information has been obtained from printed and manuscript sources and from replies to a questionnaire sent to incumbents. Information sent either in the questionnaire or by letter to the Central Council for the Care of Churches, when quoted in the list, is marked *.

The original enquiry was intended to cover the parochial libraries of the Church of England only, but in 1950, the late Archbishop of Wales asked that the Church in Wales should be included. Copies of the questionnaire were therefore sent to the Archdeacons of the Church in Wales, and as a result information about three libraries in Monmouthshire and six in Wales will be found in the alphabetical list. The Report and Recommendations, however, apply only to the Church of England.

Key to abbreviations

The number in square brackets after the place-name shows the number of books now either in the library or deposited elsewhere as a coherent block. If it is known that there are books, but not known how many, a question mark takes the place of the number (e.g. Alnwick). The absence of both brackets and a number shows that there are no books now known to exist, or that they have been dispersed by sale or, in the case of Leicester and Ipswich only, that the majority of the books have

63

been acquired since the library ceased to be connected with the church.

The following abbreviations are used for books to which frequent reference is made in the list: —

Blades = W. Blades, *Books in Chains*, 1890 (unless otherwise stated).
Christie = R. C. Christie, *The old Church and School Libraries of Lancashire*. Chetham Society, New Series, vol. 7 (1885).
Life of Bray = *Life and Designs of Thomas Bray*, ed. 1808.
Streeter = B. H. Streeter, *The Chained Library*, 1931.

AINSTABLE, Cumberland [4]. 4 of the 16 volumes given in accordance with the will of Barnabas Oley, d. 1685 (see pp. 18–19) remain in the vicarage. They are the 3 volumes of Thomas Jackson's Sermons, 1637, and the Sermons of Lancelot Andrewes, 1635.

ALCESTER, Warwickshire. An S.P.C.K. library of 74 volumes (not quite the usual selection, since it included the 5 volumes of Pole's Synopsis, and cost £29 16 6) was founded in 1712. The books were sent to the Associates of Dr. Bray, c. 1870, when about 70 volumes of the Library of Anglo-Catholic Theology were substituted for them. Only these latter remain.

ALNWICK, Northumberland [?]. An S.P.C.K. library of 68 volumes was founded in 1711 and later augmented with other books: see G. Tate, *History of Alnwick*, vol. 2, 1868–9, p. 149. The books at Alnwick seem to have been transferred to the newly founded Newcastle Chapter Library in or shortly before 1889: see the Review of Libraries in 1889, among the records of the Associates of Dr. Bray. Of the original S.P.C.K. library, nos. 1, 3–8, 10–25, 27, 42–5,

47, 53, 56, 57, 60, 62, 64, 67 are recognizable in the catalogue of the Newcastle Chapter Library printed in 1890: see NEWCASTLE. At least one of these books, no. 60, Hickes's Vindication, 1706, bound with Ken's Exposition on the Church Catechism, 1703, is in the Newcastle library now; it bears an Alnwick 'Tolle lege' bookplate. The Register (no. 9) is also in the Newcastle library.

AMBERLEY, Sussex [1]. In 1865 the collection numbered 31 volumes dating between 1691 and 1728: see *Sussex Archaeological Collections*, vol. 17 (1865), p. 236, where some titles are given and a reference is made to a catalogue listing 38 volumes 'for the use of the Incumbent for the time being and his successors for ever', and to 'Accipe librum' and 'Tolle lege' bookplates in some of the books. A photograph of one of these S.P.C.K. book-plates (see p. 33) is in the Franks Collection of Book-plates in the British Museum, no. 33846. This may be the library which benefited from the clause in Dr. Thomas Bray's will, in which he bequeathed a box of books 'towards a library of Lady Blount's or Mr. Stephen Hale's nomination to a parish near Arundel in Sussex': see *Life of Bray*, p. 58. A copy of

(*a*) Langley Marish, Bucks: a general view from the Kederminster Library into the adjoining family pew. A portrait of the donor is shown inside the open cupboard door.

(*b*) The Kederminster Library at Langley Marish, showing the fine contemporary furniture. The books are contained in presses whose doors are painted with Old Testament figures and saints.

PLATE III

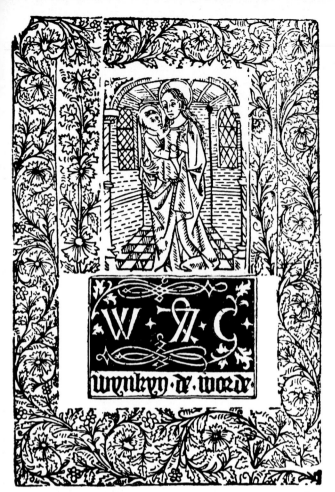

(*a*) Nantwich has a copy of the very rare Wynkyn de Worde edition of the Exposition of the Sarum Hymns and Sequences, dated 1502 (*S.T.C.* 16116a) of which this is the last page.

(*c*) Wootton Wawen, Warwickshire: seventeenth ce press, with reading desk for convenient use of the ch books it contains, in its original form before recent altera

(*b*) The seventeenth century chained library over the porch in Wimborne Minster. The chains are about 3 feet long and slide on a wrought iron rod below the shelf.

PLATE IV

Apparatus Biblicus, vol. 2, 1728, kept in the vestry seems to be the only remains of it.

ASH-BY-WROTHAM, Kent [*c.* 200]. Books 'attached to the rectory' were deposited on loan at the County Library, Maidstone, in 1947, as 'belonging to the Rector and Patron of Ash-by-Wrotham for the time being'.* Traditionally they were once part of a larger library belonging to the family of Fowler of Ash, and came to Ash Rectory in the 1860s.

ASHBY-DE-LA-ZOUCH, Leicestershire [*c.* 800]. Some books were given in 1714 and subsequent years, but most of them were bequeathed by Thomas Bate, rector of Swarkeston, d. 1727, 'for the use of the parishioners and others.' For descriptions of the library, see *Notes and Queries,* 6th Series, vol. 6 (1882), pp. 11, 52; J. P. Rylands, 'An eighteenth-century Leicestershire Church Library,' *Journal of the Ex Libris Society,* vol. 15 (1906), p. 3; W. Scott, *The Story of Ashby de la Zouch,* 1907, pp. 337–8. A copy of a typescript catalogue compiled recently by L. J. Mitchell is deposited in the Leicester Museum. Most of the books bear the name 'Tho. Bate' on the title-page.

ASKHAM, Cumberland. None of the 16 volumes given in accordance with the will of Barnabas Oley, d. 1685 (see p. 19) now survive.

ASSINGTON, Suffolk [*c.* 350]. Most of the books were 'bequeathed for the use of the parish by Thomas

Alston, Esq. (who has annotated his books very fully) in 1690.' * A contemporary list of about 300 books given by Alston is in the Bury St. Edmunds and West Suffolk Record Office, EL 5/12/1.

ASTLEY, Lancashire [*c.* 200]. The books, mainly of the sixteenth and seventeenth centuries, are now kept in the church: see Christie, pp. 69–75. In Christie's time, they were in the vicarage. He lists 27 titles (64 volumes) and says that the name 'Thomas Mort,' presumably Thomas Mort, Lord of the Manor of Astley, d. 1734, is in nearly every volume.

BAMPTON, Westmorland [*c.* 650]. An S.P.C.K. library of 67 volumes was founded in 1712. In 1751 Jonathan Tinklar, rector of Addlethorpe, Lincs., bequeathed £50, this sum to be invested in land and the interest applied 'towards the purchasing and supplying a Library to be kept and preserved for ever hereafter in the said Parish of Bampton for the particular use and benefit of the vicar there.' The interest was at one time £4 or £5 per annum, but is now £1. The Tinklar library consists of 600–700 volumes, kept in the vicarage. See M. E. Noble, *History of Bampton,* 1901, pp. 139–44; also *Charity Commissioners,* 7th Report (1822), pp. 567 –8, when the Tinklar library contained 337 volumes.

BARNSTAPLE, Devon [*c.* 350]. John Doddridge gave 112 volumes to the town in 1664, and the Mayor and Corporation built a room for them adjoining the church in 1665–7.

I

Other benefactors added to the collection which consisted of 328 volumes when it was catalogued in 1739 under the names of the donors. This old catalogue was revised by H. Luxmoore, vicar, in 1824, when there were 271 volumes. See J. R. Chanter's *Literary History of Barnstaple*, 1866, pp. 73–5, and his *Memorials of S. Peter's Church, Barnstaple*, 1881, where the 1824 catalogue is printed (pp. 166–72) and the benefactors named (p. 173). A fuller catalogue is in S. E. Dodderidge and H. G. H. Shaddick, *The Dodderidges of Devon*, 1909, pp. 42–51. The collection was transferred to the North Devon Athenaeum at Barnstaple in 1888 and thence to the Roborough Library, Exeter, in 1957.

BARTON-ON-HUMBER, S. Mary, Lincolnshire. A Terrier of 1707 at the Lincoln Diocesan Record Office lists probably 45 books. None now remain. A copy of the list was sent to the Central Council for the Care of Churches.

BASINGSTOKE, Hampshire [*c.* 110]. A library is mentioned in the accounts of the church for 1703–5 and for 1707, when a catalogue was made. In 1724 Sir George Wheler, vicar 1685–94, bequeathed his Divinity Books for the use of the vicar and the clergy of the diocese. The collection consists now of about 110 volumes, a list of which was sent to the Central Council for the Care of Churches. See F. J. Baigent and J. E. Millard, *History of Basingstoke*, 1889, pp. 527–30.

BASSINGBOURNE, Cambridgeshire [*c.* 800]. A tablet in the vestry records that Edward Nightingale of Kneesworth Hall founded the library in 1717. The books were added to by two eighteenth-century vicars, Gilbert Negus and John Williams. For a stray book, see *Notes and Queries*, vol. 8 (1853), p. 274.

BATH, Somerset [*c.* 300]. A library was begun in the church, *c.* 1619, by Arthur Lake, bishop of Bath and Wells, who gave the works of King James. It now consists of about 300 volumes, and has been transferred on extended loan to the Corporation of Bath. It is housed in two Chippendale cases in the vestibule of the Municipal Library, and is catalogued in the catalogue of the Reference Library. A catalogue of the benefactors on parchment, begun in the first half of the seventeenth century and maintained until 1715, and a mid-seventeenth century list of the books are kept with the collection. A full catalogue in manuscript compiled by W. M. Wright, librarian, in 1953, is in the library. It includes a list of 78 books listed in the Benefactors' Book, but now missing. See *Proceedings of the Library Association, 1878* (1879), p. 128, and *Notes and Queries,* 6th Series, vol. 6 (1882), p. 418.

BECCLES, Suffolk [148]. A library was formed probably *c.* 1700 by gifts from various benefactors (cf. *Notes and Queries*, vol. 8 (1853), p. 62). In the 'Notitia Parochialis' of 1705 (see p. 22), the rector reports, 'There is a library setling by the Minister there' (no. 962). *A Catalogue* *of the Beccles Church Library* was printed in 1840 and lists 148 volumes, mostly in Latin (and all, except five, earlier than 1700): a typed copy of this list was sent to the Central Council for the Care of Churches. In the same year the library was moved from the church to the Beccles Public Library, the rector and churchwardens stipulating that 'The books be open to all the inhabitants of Beccles for inspection and perusal.' After the closing of the Public Library, the books were returned to the church.

BEDFORD, [*c.* 550]. A library was founded in 1700 'by the Contributions of the Gentry and Clergy' and was settled by deed, dated 20 October 1704, 'for the use of the rector of S. John's and his successors and also of the present and all future contributors and benefactors to the value of 10s.,' who could borrow books. There were more than 130 trustees. The books were kept first at S. John's Church, and from 1748 to 1831, at S. Paul's Church, and were then deposited in the care of the Bedford Literary and Scientific Institute and General Library. The library's copy of Caxton's Ryal Book was sold at Sotheby's, 17 March 1902, lot 897, and is now in the Pierpont Morgan Library: its binding leaves, taken from two copies of an Indulgence printed by Caxton in 1481, were lots 985–6 in the same sale, and are now in the Pierpont Morgan and British Museum libraries; see S. de Ricci, *Census of Caxtons,* 1909, pp. 69, 89. Seven other printed books and four medieval manuscripts were sold at Sotheby's, 15 June 1904, lots 447–57;

three of the manuscripts, lots 455–7, are now respectively British Museum Add. 36984, 36983 and Manchester, Rylands lat. 176. Bunyan's copy of Foxe's Book of Martyrs was sold in 1910. The books that remained in 1946, about 550 volumes, some of them in bad condition, were then handed over to Bedford Corporation as a public trust, and are now housed in the John Bunyan room of the Public Library. Most of them have 'E Bibliotheca Bedfordiensi' on the title page. *A Catalogue of Books in the Library at Bedford* was printed in 1706 and there are catalogues in manuscript of the early eighteenth century (listing 822 volumes) and of 1807 (listing 703 volumes). The books were also listed on pp. 235–72 of a *Catalogue of the Circulating and Reference Libraries of the Old Library founded in 1700,* published for the Literary and Scientific Institute in 1892. For notices of the library, see the introduction to the Institute's Catalogue; T. A. Blyth, *History of Bedford,* 1873, pp. 166–7; *Gentleman's Magazine,* 1817, pt. 2, pp. 135 –6, 578; *Bedfordshire Notes and Queries,* vol. 3 (1891), p. 249.

BEETHAM, Westmorland [*c.* 150]. William Hutton, vicar of Beetham, gave about 150 volumes in 1795 'for the use of the Vicar and Curate, the School Master and the Churchwardens.' They are listed from a notebook of Hutton's, *The Beetham Repository,* Cumberland and Westmorland Antiquarian and Archaeological Society, Tract Series, no. 7 (1906), pp. 157–9. A few more books were added later.

BEVERLEY, S. Mary, Yorkshire [32]. The library was inaugurated with the gift of Walton's Polyglot in 1699. 446 volumes, given in the next ten years mainly by Thomas Alured of Beverley in 1701 and 1708 and by Charles Warton of Beverley, are recorded in an early catalogue belonging to the church. Another catalogue is among Diocesan Records at York. A lively account of the state of the library in 1856 and 1863 is in *Notes and Queries,* 3rd Series, vol. 5 (1864), p. 51: see also 6th Series, vol. 6 (1882), p. 294. In 1856 the books were used to light the church fires. Thirty-two books in bad condition now remain. A list of them was sent to the Central Council for the Care of Churches by Miss M. Johnson.

BEWDLEY, Worcestershire [over 3,000]. Thomas Wigan of Bewdley, d. 1819, bequeathed 'to the rector of Ribbesford and to the master of the Free Grammar School at Bewdley for the time being and their successors for ever, all my books which at the time of my death I may be possessed of at Bewdley aforesaid, in trust for the use of the clergy and other respectable inhabitants of that town and neighbourhood as a public library': see *Charity Commissioners,* 26th Report (1833), p. 562. The books could be lent out. The collection of over 3,000 items, much of which belonged to Wigan's father and grandfather, was kept in the Grammar School and elsewhere in Bewdley until 1950, when it was transferred on loan to Birmingham University Library. A catalogue was printed by Sir Thomas Phillipps at Middlehill in 1859 and there is a full typescript catalogue by Paul Morgan of Birmingham University Library, compiled in 1955.

BICESTER, Oxfordshire. 'A Catalogue of the Parochial Library of Burcester, 5 Octr 1757' in the Bodleian Library (MS. Oxf. Archd. Papers, Oxon. b. 22, ff. 249–52) lists 128 titles. Probably this collection belonged to the Grammar School which was housed in a room adjoining the church. J. C. Blomfield, *History of Bicester,* 1884, p. 34, refers to the destruction of this room at the restoration of the church in 1862, and says that the books were then placed in the care of one of the churchwardens. He refers to a catalogue of 1691, listing 150 books and 71 benefactors. There was no library 'worth notice' according to the incumbent in 1705 ('Notitia Parochialis,' no. 237). No books remain.

BILSTON, Staffordshire. John Tomkys, vicar of Snitterfield, Warwickshire, by will dated 14 June 1703, left his books to the minister of Bilston and desired that a catalogue of them should be 'Registered in parchment . . . that a view may be made upon the Removeall of every Minister that they may not be alienated from the Uses intended.' A copy of the will was entered by Richard Ames, curate of Bilston, in the parish register (ed. *Bilston Parish Register,* Staffordshire Parish Registers Society, 1938, pp. 220–1). In the 'Notitia Parochialis' of 1705 (see p. 22), no. 1133, Ames notes that the library 'is now in my possession.' G. T. Lawley, *History of Bilston,* 1893, p. 238, quotes a table formerly in the church, according to which Ames, who died in 1730, 'by his last will, left his Lib. of Bks., for the use of the Cur^ts of B. for ever.'

BIRMINGHAM, S. Martin [12+]. Thomas Hall, d. 1665 (cf. KING'S NORTON), gave books to form a library for the use of the ministers of Birmingham, as appears from the terms of his will. The will, dated 1664, and 'A Catalogue of those books wch are given to the library at Birmingham 1661' are in Baxter MS. Treatises 9 in Dr. Williams's Library, Gordon Square, London. The catalogue was printed thence by F. J. Powicke in *Bulletin of the John Rylands Library,* vol. 8 (1924), pp. 186–190 (299 entries). This collection of books became part of the Governors' Library at King Edward's School, Birmingham, and the remains of it are now housed with that library in the Reference Library of Birmingham Public Library.

BIRMINGHAM, S. Philip, Warwickshire [415]. A library 'free to all clergymen in the Church of England in the town and neighbourhood' was founded by the first rector, William Higgs, in 1733, and was housed after 1792 in a special room adjoining the parsonage house in S. Philip's churchyard: see W. Hutton, *History of Birmingham,* 1795, p. 357, and R. K. Dent, writing on 'Birmingham: its libraries and its booksellers,' *Book Auction Records,* vol. 4 (1906–7). A catalogue printed in 1795 lists 550 volumes. 415 volumes, all that then remained, were transferred to the Reference Library of Birmingham Public Library in 1927 and are listed in the official Donation Book of the library. A bookplate is

shown in the *Journal of the Ex Libris Society,* vol. 12 (1903), p. 79.

BISHOPS LYDEARD, Somerset. John Geale, vicar, bequeathed by will proved 22 December 1733 'my books to remain in the library that I have erected in the parish church of Bishops Liddeard': see *Notes and Queries,* vol. 154 (1928), p. 123. No books remain.

BLOXHAM, Oxfordshire [c. 40]. Books of the seventeenth and eighteenth centuries, including a once chained and now very dilapidated copy of Foxe's Book of Martyrs.

BOLSTERSTONE, Yorkshire. An S.P.C.K. library of 72 volumes was founded in 1711.

BOLTON-LE-MOORS, Lancashire [56]. The 108 books selected for the church in accordance with the will of Humphrey Chetham, d. 1653 (see MANCHESTER), were listed in 1668 and chained then 'in Mr. Chethams Chappell in the Deske there prepared for them.' The list is printed by Christie, pp. 51–5. The surviving books were transferred to Bolton School between 1836 and 1855 and are now chained in a bookcase presented to the school in 1694 (see Christie, p. 119). 'The library is a proud possession of the school and is well looked after.' * For photographs of the bookcase open and closed, see Streeter, pp. 300–1, and Christie, frontispiece.

BOSTON, Lincolnshire [c. 1500]. One of the orders made by Sir Nathaniel Brent as commissary of Archbishop Laud in his visitation, 20

August 1634, required that 'the room over the porch . . . shall be repaired and decently fitted to make a library in which to keep books given to the use of the parish' (Laud's *Works*, ed. 1847–60, vol. 5, p. 499). According to Pishey Thompson, *History of Boston*, 1856, p. 187, this was done at the request of the vicar, Anthony Tuckney, who himself gave many books. Other books were bought with money subscribed. In 1719 the Corporation paid £50 for the books of Edward Kelsall, vicar, and added them to the library. Catalogues were made in 1724 and in 1819, when over 150 volumes were sold. There are now about 1,500 volumes. For the recent restoration of the library, see *Times Literary Supplement*, vol. 49 (1950), p. 192.

BRADFIELD, Yorkshire [49]. Books were bequeathed by Robert Turie, incumbent, d. 1720 'unto the Minister of Bradfield Chapel . . . and to his successors there' (J. Eastwood, *History of Ecclesfield*, 1862, p. 337). The testator directed that a catalogue of the books should be made and entered in the Archbishop's Register at York, 'to prevent their being embezzled.' A list of them (149 titles) 'as they existed May 23 1859' is printed by Eastwood, pp. 541–5; see also Eastwood in *Notes and Queries*, 2nd Series, vol. 7 (1859), p. 473. The 49 surviving books have been catalogued recently.

BRATTON FLEMING, Devon. A monument in the chancel records that Bartholomew Wortley, rector, d. 1749, aged 97, bequeathed 'Biblio-

thecam et supellectilem omnem futuris huius ecclesiae rectoribus in perpetuum.' (Noticed in Bodleian MS. Top. Devon c. 8, f. 94; cf. Shore in *Proceedings of the Library Association* 1878, 1879, p. 145.)

BRENT ELEIGH, Suffolk. 'Dr. Colman, fellow of Trinity College, Cambridge, about 1700, built a fine parochial library at the end of the chancel of the church and well furnished it with books' (W. A. Copinger, *Manors of Suffolk*, vol. 1 (1905), p. 43): the founder was therefore Henry, son of Richard Colman of Brent Eleigh, fellow of Trinity 1694, D.D., 1712, d. 1715. The library is said to have consisted of about 1,500 books and was housed from 1859 in a small building in the churchyard (H. R. Barker, *West Suffolk Illustrated*, 1907). H. W. Tompkins saw it (*In Constable's Country*, 1906, pp. 177–8) but it seems to have disappeared before Horace Kennedy became rector in 1928. There were eight medieval manuscripts, most of which had belonged to Fane Edge (d. at Lavenham in 1727), and a volume of collections by Nicholas Roscarrock (d. 1634?). Two of these manuscripts were in a Sotheby sale 26 July 1887, lots 104 (now Bodleian Lat. liturg. f. 5, Queen Margaret's Gospels) and 268 (now Cambridge University Library, Add. 3327); six were acquired by Cambridge University Library in 1891 (Add. MSS. 3037–42); one was acquired by the Fitzwilliam Museum in 1891 (MS. 17); cf. M. R. James and A. Jessopp, *Life and Miracles of St. William of Norwich*, 1896, p. 1 and M. R. James, *Eton and King's*,

1926, pp. 205–6. An eighteenth-century catalogue of the library, lot 304 in the 1887 sale, went to E. Parsons for 1s.

B R E W O O D, Staffordshire. An S.P.C.K. library of 72 volumes was founded in 1710. Nothing of it now remains.

B R I D G N O R T H, S. Leonard, Shropshire [*c.* 3,000]. The library was founded by Hugh Stackhouse, master of the Free Grammar School and rector of Oldbury, d. 1743, who bequeathed his 'Study of Books and Pamphletts' to the Society of Clergymen in and about Bridgnorth. The deed of foundation, 1 July 1743, includes a list of about 1,500 books and some pamphlets : a nineteenth-century copy of it is British Museum MS. Add. 28732, ff. 13–21. The library was a subscription library in the nineteenth century, when many books were added to it. The Bodleian copy of the *Rules and Catalogue of the Stackhouse Library, Bridgnorth,* 1838, contains printed additions to 1846 (pp. 32–44) and corrections and additions in manuscript. Thomas Lyttleton of Bridgnorth bequeathed £30 in 1792, the interest of which was to provide for the upkeep of the books and of the library-room attached to S. Leonard's Church (British Museum MS. Add. 28732, f. 24).

B R I D L I N G T O N, Yorkshire [59]. An S.P.C.K. library of 72 volumes was founded in 1710 : 46 volumes remain (nos. 1, 3–8, 10–13, 15–21, 26–9, 31, 35–44, 47, 50, 52, 55, 58, 60, 61, 63–5, 67, 69, 70),

together with 8 volumes of *Critici Sacri,* Amsterdam, 1698, given by the Associates of Dr. Bray in 1871. The cupboard in which the S.P.C.K. library was sent to Bridlington is still in the church : see pl. I (*a*). There are also in the church 5 volumes of the seventeenth century, formerly, no doubt, chained to a desk, but kept now in an exhibition case.

B R I S T O L, All Saints [8]. Five early printed books (1503 and earlier) and 3 medieval manuscripts. The printed books have been together since early in the sixteenth century to judge from the script of titles written on the fore-edges, and one of the manuscripts contains a Bristol document in the binding. It seems not impossible that these books may have been at All Saints' since before the Reformation. They are described briefly by T. W. Williams, 'Gloucestershire Mediaeval Libraries,' *Transactions of the Bristol and Gloucestershire Archaeological Society,* vol. 31 (1908), pp. 88–90.

B R O M H A M, Bedfordshire [*c.* 800]. The library was founded by Thomas, 2nd Baron Trevor, in 1740 and added to later by members of the Trevor family. It consists of about 800 volumes in a room above the church porch. Three eighteenth-century catalogues in manuscript are kept with it. The charms of the library are celebrated by Robert Hampden-Trevor, 4th Baron Trevor, in his Latin poem *Villa Bromhamensis* (cf. *Notes and Queries,* 6th Series, vol. 6 (1882), p. 258). A copy of his poetical works, printed at the Bodoni Press at Parma in 1792 (see H. C. Brooks, *Compendiosa Bibliografia di Edizione Bodoniane,* Florence, 1927, no. 470), is in the library.

BROMSGROVE, Worcestershire [*c.* 100]. The books, mainly seventeenth century, have been listed in print by W. A. Cotton, *Bromsgrove Church,* 1881, pp. 39–41, and thence in *The Bibliographer,* vol. 1 (1881), p. 134. Many belonged to Thomas Tullie.

BROOKTHORPE, Gloucestershire. An S.P.C.K. library of 72 volumes was founded in 1712. No books remain.

BROUGHTON, Huntingdonshire [*c.* 600 + pamphlets]. Most of the books bear either the name or the ex-donor of William Torkington (rector of Wistow, Hunts, d. 1737), or the name of Robert Hodson, rector 1713 –74. Some are in bad condition. The sequestrator informed the Central Council in 1950 that the books had been sorted by Dr. R. H. Murray, rector 1922–8, and that 'those of no consequence were disposed of.' * For the sale of this library in 1958, see Addenda, p. 112.

BUBWITH, Yorkshire [c. 7]. James Raine refers on p. xvii of the preface to his *Catalogue of the Printed Books in the Library of the Dean and Chapter of York,* 1896, to the existence of a catalogue 'properly engrossed on parchment' of a large collection of books bequeathed to Bubwith. This catalogue, dated April 1747, is now in the library of York

Minster (BB. 10. 1). Raine himself saw some of these books 'some thirty years ago . . . in a tattered and neglected condition.' He says that they were used to light the vestry fires, until 'the sole remnant of some six or seven hundred volumes were some six or eight,' which the incumbent 'picked up in the village and wisely offered to the Dean and Chapter of York for preservation in their library.' Three of these have been identified in the York library : see Raine's catalogue, pp. 8, 142, 284 (Alstedius, Douza, Malcolm).

BURGH-BY-SANDS, Cumberland. The books bequeathed under the will of Barnabas Oley (see p. 19) and the S.P.C.K. library of 72 volumes founded in 1712 (see p. 38) are now missing.

BURY, Lancashire. For the library of 600 books and more given 'for the use of Bury parish,' by Henry Bury before his death in 1638, see Christie, pp. 139–42. Christie notes that two books with Bury's name and one with his initials survive at Bury School. The tradition at Bury in 1705 ('Notitia Parochialis' (see p. 22), no. 219) was that Henry Bury's gift was to the school (which he founded) and that the best of the books had been stolen in the Civil War.

BURY ST. EDMUNDS, Suffolk [*c.* 475]. The library was begun in 1595 and contained nearly 200 volumes in 1599 when a catalogue was drawn up (S. Jayne, *Library Catalogues of the English Renaissance,* 1956, p. 87; *Notes and Queries,* 6th Series, vol. 2 (1883), p. 117). It now contains about

475 volumes, some of which have suffered from damp. C. M. Neale made a catalogue in 1911 and gave an account of the library in the *S. James' Parish Magazine* for 1911, nos. 344–6. The books printed before 1700 have been included in Miss Margaret Hands's Cathedral Libraries catalogue. Two of the 4 medieval manuscripts are noticed briefly by M. R. James, *On the Abbey of S. Edmund at Bury*, Cambridge Antiquarian Society, Octavo Series, vol. 28 (1895), pp. 50, 53, 67; and all 4 briefly in *Historical Manuscripts Commission*, 14th Report, App., pt. 8, pp. 121–2. See pl. I (*b*).

BUSHEY, Hertfordshire. A library of eighteenth-century (?) books was an heirloom in the rectory until soon after 1943. About half the books, mostly sermons, and many 'damp and dilapidated' were then destroyed, and the rest, largely canon law, were given to the Community of the Resurrection at Mirfield, Yorks.* These books have not been identified in the library at Mirfield.

CAERLEON, Monmouthshire [?]. A number of eighteenth-century books labelled 'Caerleon Parochial Lending Library' are now in the library of Llandaff Cathedral.

CARTMEL, Lancashire [*c.* 300]. The books, with a few exceptions (see Christie, pp. 76–7) were bequeathed by Thomas Preston of Holker, d. 1697 'to be placed in the new vestry.' They were catalogued in 1698 (extracts by Christie, pp. 82–93): a typescript copy of this catalogue was sent to the Central Council for the Care of Churches. A new catalogue of the collection by David Ramage forms part of a paper by Canon S. Taylor, 'The Library in Cartmel Priory Church,' *Transactions of the Cumberland and Westmorland Antiquarian and Archaeological Society,* New Series, vol. 55 (1956), pp. 213–46.

CASTLETON, Derbyshire [*c.* 550]. A brass plaque in the chancel is inscribed '1819. The Books deposited here are a Gift to the Parish from the late Vicar The Revᵈ F. Farran. They are to be lent at the Discretion of the Vicar.' The collection was augmented later by Farran's brother-in-law, G. J. Hamilton. His books and Farran's contain their respective book-plates, and Farran's are mostly marked also, in gilt letters on the covers, 'Parish Library Castleton.' There are two catalogues in manuscript and a borrowers' book begun in 1852, but little used after 1866. Notices of the library are in *Notes and Queries*, vol. 8 (1853), p. 369, in the *Report from the Select Committee on Public Libraries,* 1849, p. 221, and in J. C. Cox, *Churches of Derbyshire,* vol. 2, 1877, p. 133.

CHELMSFORD, Essex [*c.* 2,000]. About 400 of the volumes housed in a room over the south porch of the Parish Church (now the Cathedral) belonged to John Knightsbridge, D.D., d. 1677, and were given by his brother Anthony in 1679 'in usum vicinorum theologorum'; the rest are later additions. A careful and detailed catalogue of many of the books in quarto and smaller sizes compiled by

73

Andrew Clark, c. 1904, is now Bod-leian MS. Eng. misc. c. 42–3. Some notes by Clark on these books are in *Essex Review,* vol. 12 (1903), pp. 238 –42. A manuscript catalogue is noticed in *Notes and Queries,* 6th Series, vol. 6 (1882), p. 15.

CHEPSTOW, Monmouthshire. An S.P.C.K. library of 72 volumes was founded in 1712. Nothing of it now remains.

CHIPPENHAM, Cambridge-shire. 'A good Collection of Books in the Chapel, at the East End of the South Isle' is mentioned by Francis Blomefield, *Collectanea Cantabrigien-sia,* 1750, p. 194. No books remain.

CHIRBURY, Shropshire [180]. The library consists mainly of books bequeathed by Edward Lewis, vicar, d. 1677, who asked that they should be placed in the schoolhouse built by him in the churchyard, 'for the Use of the Schoolmaster or any other of the Parishioners who shall desire to read them' (see *Transactions of the Shropshire Archaeological Society,* 3rd Series, vol. 6 (1906), p. 354). It is noticed in the 'Notitia Parochialis' of 1705 (see p. 22), no. 357. A list of the books taken 10 February 1859 is printed in *Trans. Shropshire Arch. Soc.,* vol. 8 (1885), pp. 119–21: see also *Notes and Queries,* 12th Series, vol. 12 (1923), p. 495, and Streeter, pp. 293–4. The books are now kept in the vicarage. They were formerly chained and many have had their chains reattached to them.

CODDENHAM, Suffolk [?]. 'A

small collection of books left for the use of the Rectors of Coddenham and their successors, and housed in the Rectory.' *

COLEORTON, Leicestershire [c. 500]. The books were at the rectory until recently, but at present are packed in boxes and in the care of the Secretary, Church House, Leicester.

COLESHILL, Warwickshire. In 1730 Dr. Thomas Bray bequeathed 31 folio volumes of Aquinas and Lorinus (cf. *Life of Bray,* p. 58). No books remain.

COMPTON, Surrey. Charles Kerry recorded, c. 1870, that 'the remains of an old library were pre-served in the upper story of the church,' before its restoration. When he wrote, the larger books had been lost, but nearly 30 smaller books in a very tattered and imperfect condi-tion were kept at the rectory, includ-ing J. Mollerus, *Fasciculus Reme-diorum,* Bas., 1579, *Dormi Secure,* and a book which had belonged to Edward Fulham (of Eastbury Manor) in the seventeenth century (Derby Public Library, Kerry MSS., vol. 2, p. 136: reference supplied by T. E. C. Walker in 1950). No books remain now.

CONISTON, Lancashire. Roger Fleming of Coniston Hall gave money in 1699 and bequeathed money in 1703, out of which 8s. 4d. was set aside annually for buying books. In 1885 there were about 100 books, which 'are, or were formerly, lent out at Easter to any of the inhabitants who wished to read them.' See Christie, pp. 95–6, and see also *Charity Commissioners,* 3rd Report (1820), p. 224. The books were destroyed, probably in 1957, as being dirty and unread.

CORBRIDGE, Northumberland. 12 books of divinity and 7 prayer books were sent by Mrs. Alice Colpitts of Newcastle in 1729 'to be put in the church for the use of the parishioners in common for every person.' The books were listed in the parish register and thence in *Notes and Queries,* vol. 10 (1854), p. 213, and in *History of Northumberland,* vol. 10, 1914, p. 217.

CORSTON, Somerset. An S.P.C.K. library of 67 volumes was founded in 1710. The books were sent to the Associates of Dr. Bray in 1869 at the request of the Secretary of the Associates, but reluctantly. Correspondence on the subject is entered in the original Library Register remaining at Corston and in the archives of the Associates of Dr. Bray.

COSTOCK, Nottinghamshire. Henry Twisden, rector, records in the 'Notitia Parochialis' of 1705 (see p. 22), no. 641, that his immediate predecessor, Thomas Townsend, d. 1701, 'gave a considerable library wch he had in ye Parsonage House for ye use of his successors, Rectors of Costock for ever,' and ordered that 3 catalogues should be made, one for the Archiepiscopal Registry in York, one for the Archidiaconal Registry in Nottingham, and one for the patrons of the church. He notes that the

books 'with ye Press wch contains y^{em}' were then in his possession. In 1887 the library was no longer to be found (J. T. Godfrey, *Churches of Nottinghamshire, Hundred of Rushcliffe,* 1887, p. 71).

CRANFIELD, Bedfordshire. A Terrier of 1715 at the Bedford County Record Office records 'a small parochial library.' No books remain.

CREDITON, Devon [1250]. Most of the books were bequeathed to the Governors of the church by Thomas Ley, vicar 1689–1721, for the use of his successors. They were repaired with the aid of a grant from the Pilgrim Trust in 1950 (see 20th Report, pp. 36–7). A catalogue was made by Miss Margaret Hands in 1949.

CROSBY ON EDEN, Cumberland. None of the 16 books given in accordance with the will of Barnabas Oley, d. 1685 (see p. 19), now remain.

CROSBY RAVENSWORTH, Westmorland. None of the 16 books given in accordance with the will of Barnabas Oley, d. 1685 (see p. 19), now remain.

CRUNDALE, Kent [c. 900]. A catalogue, Canterbury Cathedral MS. Y4.31, is headed 'A Catalogue of Books left by the Reverend Richard Forster A.M. Rector of Crundale to his Successors in the said living for ever.' Another catalogue, Canterbury Cathedral Y.4.30, independent of

Y. 4. 31 and headed 'Crundall library 1728,' was deposited at Canterbury in 1729, the year in which Forster died. The catalogues list 195 folios, 161 quartos, and 494 octavos and give dates and, sometimes, places of printing. About 900 volumes now belong to the library and are housed at Godmersham Vicarage.

CUDWORTH, Somerset. Nothing is known of the books bequeathed by Richard Busby, rector 1639–c. 1648, in 1695 for the use of the minister and his successors for ever: see G. F. R. Barker, *Memoir of Richard Busby,* 1895, p. 143.

DALSTON, Cumberland [9]. 8 of the 16 books given in accordance with the will of Barnabas Oley, d. 1685 (see p. 19), remain in the vicarage. They are two volumes of Hammond and nos. 5–7, 9–11; also R. Fiddes, *Theologica Practica,* 1720.

DARLINGTON, Co. Durham [over 60]. An S.P.C.K. library of 72 volumes was founded in 1711. 49 of these volumes remain (nos. 1, 3–10, 12–14, 16–25, 27, 31, 33–40, 42–6, 48, 50, 52–5, 58, 60, 63–5, 68) including the Register (no. 9) and with them are a dozen other seventeenth and eighteenth century books, and a collection of books on local history.

DAROWEN, Montgomeryshire [over 52]. An S.P.C.K. library of 67 volumes was founded in 1710. 52 volumes remain (nos. 2–5, 7, 8, 10–13, 15–24, 26–38, 41–5, 47–51, 53–4, 56–60, 63, 64) in the rectory, together with some later books. A

book-plate from one of the S.P.C.K. books is reproduced in the report of the Associates of Dr. Bray for 1944 and some other years.

DEARHAM, Cumberland. None of the 16 books given in accordance with the will of Barnabas Oley, d. 1685 (see p. 19), now remain.

DENCHWORTH, Berkshire [150]. The incumbent records in the 'Notitia Parochialis' of 1705 (see p. 22), no. 1244, 'Over the Portch of yᵉ said Church the worshipful Gregory Geering Esq. yᵉ present Lord of yᵉ Manner and Patron of yᵉ said Church did in the year 1693 erect a small Library and endow'd it with a considerable number of yᵉ best Modern Authors for yᵉ use of yᵉ Vicars for ever. And Mʳ Edward Brewster Citizen and Stationer of the City of London seconded his Benefaction with a bountiful Donation of several valuable Books to yᵉ said Library.' Inscriptions in the books record these gifts and also those of Ralph Kedden, vicar 1691–1720, 'to his successors . . . for ever.' A careful catalogue by C. H. Tomlinson, with notes of donors, was printed as a *Supplement to the Denchworth Annual,* 1875: of this the Bodleian has a copy. An 'erring vicar' (cf. Blades, p. 21), sold a copy of Caxton's Golden Legend to the Oxford bookseller Parker in 1843. Parker sold it to the Bodleian in 1848 for £20: it is now Arch. G. b. 2. See also *Notes and Queries,* 6th Series, vol. 4 (1881), p. 304.

DETLING, Kent. An S.P.C.K.

library of 72 volumes was founded in 1710. The books were sold for £1, *c.* 1875. 'A catalogue of the Parochial Library at Debtling' is in Canterbury Cathedral MS. Y. 4. 30, pp. 141–3.

DODDINGTON, Kent [*c.* 385]. 364 books, the library of Daniel Somerscales, vicar 1694–1737, were given by his executor, Samuel Lisle, archdeacon of Canterbury, in 1743. A 'catalogue of the Books in the Parochial Library,' compiled at this time, remains at Doddington, together with a later catalogue. It lists 71 folios, 30 quartos, and 263 octavos, and gives dates and usually places of printing. Catalogues dated 1744 and 1774 are in the Kent County Archives Office, Maidstone : see F. Hull, *Guide to the Kent County Archives Office,* 1958, pp. 116, 118. Some books were given in the early nineteenth century by J. Radcliffe, vicar. The library is in the vicarage. Some early-nineteenth-century notes on it are in Canterbury Cathedral Add. MS. 21, f. 4.

DONCASTER, Yorkshire. The 'Society's Library,' founded in 1714 by a society of local clergy and erected as a 'common public library' by a deed of settlement in 1726, contained several hundred volumes dated between 1517 and 1724. The library was over the south porch of the parish church and was destroyed with the church by fire in 1853. The list of the books in E. Miller, *History of Doncaster,* 1804, pp. 98–102, is taken from the schedule attached to the deed of settlement. A better catalogue was printed in 1821. A Minute Book of the Society, 1714–28, and other

papers concerning it, 1714–36, are in the custody of the vicar of Doncaster. A good account of the library by J. Ballinger, with a list of the books printed before 1550, is in *Old Yorkshire,* vol. 3, 1882, pp. 149–54.

DONINGTON, Lincolnshire [*c.* 1500]. John Wilson, vicar, d. 1869, gave about 1,500 volumes, which are now kept in the vicarage. A list of 17 books printed before 1700 was sent to the Central Council for the Care of Churches.

DORCHESTER, All Saints, Dorset. An S.P.C.K. library of 67 volumes was founded in 1710. Nothing of it now remains.

DUDLESTON, Shropshire [62]. An S.P.C.K. library of 72 volumes was founded in 1712. Nos. 1–6, 8, 11–21, 23, 25–6, 28, 30–48, 50–60, 62–70, 72 remain in the vicarage.

DULLINGHAM, Cambridgeshire. An S.P.C.K. library of 72 volumes was founded in 1712. Nothing of it now remains.

DURHAM, S. Oswald. In 1701 John Cock, vicar, deprived 1689, bequeathed his books to his successors, the vicars of S. Oswald's, and £20 to build a place for their reception (R. Surtees, *History of Durham,* vol. 4, pt. 2, 1840, p. 83). These books were sold without permission in the time of Alexander Dunn, vicar 1929–39. Previously 3 incunabula had been listed by E. V. Stocks in *Durham University Journal,* vol. 22 (1919),

p. 57 (nos. 191, 226, 252) and references to 144 'S.T.C. books' had been included in the *Short Title Catalogue*. There is a list of 80 other *S.T.C.* books at Durham University Library, which also possesses a few books from the library. According to a report by E. V. Stocks in 1922 (MS. at Durham University Library), the old catalogue recorded 1,578 volumes.

EARL STERNDALE, Derbyshire. James Hill bequeathed books by will proved at York, 11 June 1712 (vol. 68, f. 66). In 1823 there were 24 books of this gift in a cupboard beside the altar; the names of the books were written on the cupboard doors (J. C. Cox, *Churches of Derbyshire,* vol. 2, 1877, p. 486, quoting an account by R. R. Rawlins).

EAST HARLSEY, Yorkshire [*c.* 600]. Books were bequeathed by George Lawson, d. 1725, 'for the benefit of the curate of East Harlsey and his successors for ever.' They are kept in the rectory. There is a manuscript catalogue.

ECCLESFIELD, Yorkshire [2]. 13 'Bookes Chayned in the Church,' some of which appear to have been given in 1549 by Charles Parsons, vicar (see J. Eastwood, *History of Ecclesfield,* 1862, p. 517), are listed in church accounts for 1606 and are recorded as having been rebound by 'Mr. Crofte Bookebinder' in 1638. The list is printed by Eastwood, pp. 175–6 and also, thence, by Blades, p. 23. Blades was informed that the books were very dilapidated and had been removed from the chancel in

1860. Four of them remain, bound in 2 volumes.

EFFINGHAM, Surrey [2]. A library was bequeathed to his successors by John Miller, vicar, d. 1724: see O. Manning and W. Bray, *History of Surrey,* vol. 2, 1809, pp. 714–15. A note-book of Miller's and one book (Sermons of Ralph Brownrigg, ed. W. Martyn, 1664) inscribed 'The Gift of Mr Miller to the Vicars of Effingham in Surrey for ever' remain at the vicarage. The rest of the library was sold by E. F. Bayly, vicar 1882–1929.

ELHAM, Kent [*c.* 1,200]. A collection bequeathed by Lee Warly, d. 1809, to the vicar and churchwardens on behalf of the parishioners of Elham. Three quarters of them are at present at Elham Church and one quarter in the library of Canterbury Cathedral.

ELMLEY. See PERSHORE.

ELSTON, Nottinghamshire [*c.* 24]. Some books belonging to John South, rector 1702–32, survived in the rectory until a few years ago, when they were handed over on deposit to the County Librarian, County Hall, Trent Bridge, Nottingham.

EVESHAM, Worcestershire. An S.P.C.K. library of 67 volumes was founded in 1710. None of them now remain, but the upper half of the original book-cupboard is still in the church. It contains a catalogue on the inside of the door and is marked outside with the number '32.' This is the number of the library assigned to

Evesham by the Committee of S.P.C.K.

F E C K E N H A M, Worcestershire [c. 80]. An S.P.C.K. library of 72 volumes was founded in 1712. 69 of these volumes remain, together with a dozen other pre-1800 books. A list was sent to the Central Council for the Care of Churches.

F E R S F I E L D, Norfolk. The only evidence for the existence of this library comes from a book-plate in the Franks Collection at the British Museum (no. 33852), printed evidently on Francis Blomefield's private press and inscribed:
'This Book belongeth to the Parish Church of St. Andrew in Fersfield, Anno Dom. 1736
    Francis Blomefield, Rector
    Mr. Timothy Coleman ⎫   Ch.
    Mr. Robert Algar, Jun.⎰ Wardens
      Fersfield: Printed, 1736'

F I N E D O N, Northamptonshire [c. 1,000]. A brief hand-list of the books preserved at Finedon, begins with the words 'On the 21st Day of September 1788 . . . the Cell over the South Porch was dedicated for the Purpose of a Theological and Ecclesiastical Library for the (sole *interlined*) Use of the Ministers of Finedon for ever, the Foundation Book being Dr Thos Bray's Bibliotheca Parochialis.' The founder is said to have been Sir John English Dolben, F.S.A., d. 1837, and most of the books bear the armorial book-plate of his grandfather 'Sir John Dolben Bar^t of Finedon in Northamptonshire,' d. 1756. See *Architectural Notes of the Archdeaconry of Northampton*, 1849, p. 136.

F L A X L E Y, Gloucestershire. An S.P.C.K. library of 72 volumes was founded in 1710. The original bookcase remains in the rectory, and there are believed to have been books in it until 1948 when they 'were sold with the effects of the Rectory.' *

F L O O K B U R G H, Lancashire [67]. An S.P.C.K. library was founded in 1725 (see p. 30). The remaining books agree with nos. 1–3, 5, 7–11, 15–21, 23–9, 32–7, 39–44, 46–51, 53, 54, 56–61, 63–73, 75, 78, 80, 81 of the books listed in the catalogue of WHITCHURCH, Hants (see p. 104), together with W. Hopkins, *Seventeen Sermons*, 1708, and J. Collier, *Several Discourses upon practical subjects*, 1726. A list of the books was sent to the Central Council for the Care of Churches.

FRISBY - ON - THE - WREAK, Leicestershire. 'Mr. Nicholas Sharp about fifty years since . . . left about 30 books' ('Notitia Parochialis' of 1705 (see p. 22), no. 761). J. Nichols, *History of Leicestershire*, vol. 3, 1800, p. 262, records this gift and mentions books, 'amongst others S. Augustine and Origen and other Fathers in a wretched condition,' in a room at the west end of the church. One Nicholas Sharp of Frisby died in 1614. Another of the name was B.A. 1641 (J. A. Venn, *Alumni Cantabrigienses*).

G I L L I N G H A M, Dorset [c. 300]. Thomas Freke bequeathed 619 volumes to the vicar and feoffees of the parish lands of Gillingham in 1718: see Canon J. M. J. Fletcher in *Proceed-*

ings of the Dorset Natural History and Antiquarian Field Club, vol. 35 (1914), p. 21. About 300 books remain in the vicarage. J. Hutchins, *History of Dorset*, vol. 3, 1868, p. 647, mentions an original list of the books appended to the deed of gift.

GORTON, Lancashire [*c.* 50]. 68 books were bought with £30 bequeathed by Humphrey Chetham, d. 1653 (see MANCHESTER), and were chained in a bookcase in 1658. Over 50 books remain and are still kept chained in the original case. A list of the books made in 1658 is printed by Christie, pp. 64–6, and an annotated catalogue of 36 of the survivors by G. J. French (with reproductions of title-pages) forms pp. 110–81 of *Bibliographical Notices of the Church Libraries at Turton and Gorton,* Chetham Society, vol. 38 (1855). A photograph of the bookcase with one side open is in Streeter, p. 303. See also pl. II (*a*) of this publication.

GRANTHAM, Lincolnshire [*c.* 250+759]. Francis Trigge, rector of Welbourn, Lincs, by a deed now in the Borough archives dated 20 October 1598, gave books to the value of 'one hundereth poundes or thereabouts' to the Alderman and Burgesses of Grantham 'for the better encreasinge of learninge . . . by such of the cleargie and others as well beinge inhabitantes in or near Grantham and the soake thereof as in other places in the said Countie,' this library to be kept chained in a 'verie convenient place in a chamber over the sowth porch' of the church. A catalogue

dated February 1609 is annexed to the deed. The books in the room over the porch now number about 250 and are mostly of Trigge's gift. 83 of them are chained. A modern list of the books and a copy of the deed and of the catalogue of 1609 have been sent to the Central Council for the Care of Churches. Photographs of the library are in Blades, pls. 5 and 6, and in Streeter, p. 298.

John Newcome, Lady Margaret Professor of Divinity at Cambridge, d. 1765, bequeathed some 700 books to the Corporation of Grantham : see E. Turnor, *History of Grantham,* 1806, p. 28. These were housed in the vestry until 1929, when they were transferred to the Grantham Public Library.

GRAVELEY, Cambridgeshire [*c.* 1,400]. According to an inscription in the church, Henry Trotter, B.D. (rector, d. 1766), bequeathed his library of 'near 1400 volumes . . . for the use of the neighbouring Clergy,' together with '£50 to build a room wherein to keep them.' The books were transferred to Jesus College, Cambridge, when the rectory was sold, and are at present in the Bursary there. The rector has a catalogue.

GREAT YARMOUTH, Norfolk [*c.* 320]. A list of the books in the library, 175 titles, was printed by H. Swinden, *History of Great Yarmouth,* 1772, pp. 886–92 : all the dates of printing are before 1700. About 50 books were seriously damaged in the last war. Until the church is rebuilt, the books are deposited in the Public Library. See E. J. Lupson,

St. Nicholas Church, Great Yarmouth, 1881, pp. 138–61 : the 2nd ed., 1897, contains on p. 142 an illustration of the ingenious six-shelf library lectern-desk, now destroyed.

HACKNESS, Yorkshire [115]. The library was erected in 1700 by Sir Philip Sydenham, d. 1739 : cf. *Victoria County History, North Riding,* vol. 2, p. 531. The Benefactors' Book begun in 1701 lists twenty names of donors in the years 1701 to 1729. The same book contains a catalogue of the books made in 1721, when there were 283 volumes, together with loose papers. A catalogue of 1862 lists the collection as it now is.

HALIFAX, Yorkshire [*c.* 300 + *c.* 400]. The library founded by Robert Clay, vicar 1624–8, and increased by later gifts has been described in two papers by T. W. Hanson, 'Halifax Parish Church,' *Transactions of the Halifax Antiquarian Society,* 1909, pp. 288–98, and 'Halifax Parish Church Library,' *ibid.,* 1951, pp. 37–47. A catalogue of 1652 printed by Hanson in 1909 (*loc. cit.,* pp. 294–6) lists 43 volumes. 251 titles are listed in a nineteenth-century catalogue, a copy of which was sent to the Central Council for the Care of Churches. About 400 books, 83 of which are earlier than 1800, were given in 1862 by William Priestley. They are kept separately.

HALTON, Cheshire [*c.* 400]. A library-room was built and furnished with 4 presses of books by Sir John Chesshyre in 1753 'pro communi literatorum usu sub cura Curati

Capellae de Halton,' according to the inscription over the door. The room and its books have been described by W. A. Axon, 'Sir John Chesshyre's Library at Halton,' in *Library Journal,* vol. 4 (1879), pp. 35–8, and by C. Nickson, *History of Runcorn,* 1887, pp. 114–7. The books were recently 'in very bad condition.'* A catalogue printed on vellum in London in 1733 is kept with them. An extract from Chesshyre's will concerning the library is in *Charity Commissioners,* 31st Report (1837), p. 749.

HATFIELD BROAD OAK, Essex [*c.* 300]. The collection was founded by George Stirling, vicar *c.* 1684–1728, and housed in a room built to receive it by Sir Charles Barrington in 1708 : see F. W. Galpin, 'Hatfield Broad Oak,' *Essex Review,* vol. 44 (1935), p. 83.

HEATHFIELD, Sussex [*c.* 230]. Richard Wilkin, bookseller of S. Paul's Churchyard, d. 1740, son of William Wilkin, vicar 1665–99, bequeathed 'the books in my press and the said press to the use of the residing Vicars of Heathfield and the Curates for ever to be kept in a dry convenient place in the Vicaridge House' : see P. Lucas, *Heathfield Memorials,* 1910, p. 26. The books are kept in the vicarage in their old cupboard. A catalogue is on the doors of the cupboard. Another catalogue, signed by William Preston, vicar 1731–71, is said to have been deposited at the Diocesan Registry in 1745.

HENLEY-IN-ARDEN, Warwickshire. An S.P.C.K. library of

L

67 volumes was founded in 1710. Nothing of it now remains.

HENLEY-ON-THAMES, Oxfordshire [c. 800].
Charles Aldrich, rector, d. 1737, bequeathed 'all my study of books to the Rectory of Henley, being desirous to lay the foundation of a Parochial Library': see J. S. Burn, *History of Henley on Thames,* 1861, pp. 103–7. *A catalogue of the Old Library at Henley-on-Thames*, was printed in 1852. In 1909 some hundreds (?) of volumes were removed to Christ Church, Oxford, and are now kept in the library there; probably all these books had previously belonged to Christ Church, and had been disposed of to Aldrich, presumably as 'duplicates.' Nine more books were taken to Christ Church in 1942: see W. G. Hiscock, *A Christ Church Miscellany,* 1946, p. 64. About 475 volumes, some in bad condition, remained at Henley until 1957, when they were transferred to Reading University Library on deposit. In 1859 a Henley Library label was put inside all the books. A manuscript catalogue of the Greek manuscripts given to the Bodleian Library by Oliver Cromwell is now in the Bodleian (*Sum. Cat.* 34477).

HEREFORD, All Saints [c. 300].
The books were mostly bequeathed by William Brewster, d. 1715. They are chained in bookcases in the Lady Chapel. There is a manuscript list of them in the Public Library and a printed list by Blades, pp. 53–9. Photographs of the bookcases are in Streeter, p. 307, in Blades, pl. 8, and below, pl. II (*c*). The library was saved by the then dean of Windsor from being sold in or about 1870: see Blades, p. 27.

HILLINGDON, Middlesex [1].
The will of Samuel Reynardson, d. 1721, includes a bequest of his books for the use of the vicar and his successors and directions that his pot-plants, etc., should be sold and a library room erected over the church porch and furnished with the proceeds (as was done) and that this library should be administered according to the rules for the preservation of parochial libraries contained in the Act of Parliament of 1709: see D. Lysons, *An Historical Account of those Parishes in the County of Middlesex which are not described in the Environs of London,* 1800, pp. 168–9. The 23 titles quoted by Lysons show that this was a valuable general library, particularly strong in books on botany. According to information received by the Central Council in 1950, the books were burnt at the direction of A. M. Bashford, vicar 1934–49, except for a copy of *Eikon Basilike,* which the verger rescued. W. E. Walford, writing in *Notes and Queries,* 6th Series, vol. 8 (1883), p. 178, says that the collection was then 'very good and well-kept.'

HULL, Holy Trinity, Yorkshire [667].
Abraham de la Pryme, d. 1704, made a catalogue of the collection and included it in his 'Short Description and Account of yᵉ Two Churches of the Holy Trinity and S. Mary's in Kingston upon Hull,' the autograph copy of which is now in the Hull Public Library: see *The Diary of*

Abraham de la Pryme, Surtees Society, vol. 54 (1870), p. 298; transcripts are British Museum, MS. Lansdowne 891 (eighteenth century), and in the Hull Public Library (nineteenth century). Entries in the church accounts noted by Pryme show that Mrs. Eleanor Crowle gave £5 in 1665 'to be disposed of in Books for ye use of the Church,' and further sums of £20 and £5 in 1666 and 1667 for the same purpose. Pryme considered her to be the foundress. John Tickell reported that the library was 'very handsome and neat' and 'continually increasing in number,' since the churchwardens had forty shillings a year to buy books at their own discretion: see J. Tickell, *History of Kingston upon Hull,* 1796, p. 793. The collection was given by the vicar and churchwardens to the Hull Museums Committee in 1907, and was transferred to University College, Hull (now University of Hull), in 1938. Many of the bindings are in a bad state. Most of them have EST (for Ecclesia Sanctae Trinitatis ?) stamped on the front cover. A typescript list of the books has been sent to the Central Council for the Care of Churches. 429 volumes are earlier than 1700. The purchases with the annual £2 from 1798 to 1860 are listed in a note-book belonging to the University Library: they include seventeenth-century editions of Basil, Justinus, Strabo, Photius, and Salmasius. A manuscript Bible with historiated initials listed by Pryme and in a catalogue of an exhibition held at the Town Hall, Hull, from the 1st to the 6th April 1899 is now missing: see the *Publishers' Circular,* no. 118 (1923), p. 306. It bore the signature of Thomas, Lord Fairfax, on the first leaf. A seventeenth-century copy of the Visitation of Yorkshire by Robert Glover, Somerset Herald, in 1584–5, with additions, remains at Holy Trinity.

HULL, S. Mary Lowgate, Yorkshire [*c.* 100]. An inventory of 1682 in the Churchwardens' Books, 1640–1716, lists 16 books (f. 49) and 11 others were given in 1694 (f. 50). The incumbent records in the 'Notitia Parochialis' of 1705 (see p. 22): 'There have been some weak efforts made towards settling a library in ye Parish, but its fallen to nought' (no. 1044). Many of the books now forming the library were bequeathed by John Scott, vicar 1817–34, and were printed after 1800.

HURLEY, Berkshire. The incumbent records in the 'Notitia Parochialis' of 1705 (see p. 22): 'Here are 27 Folios (given I believe by ye above named Sir Richard Lovelace) for ye use of ye vicar' (no. 1442). The founder was presumably the Richard Lovelace of Hurley who was knighted in 1599 and created Baron Lovelace in 1627. He died in 1634.

IPSWICH, Suffolk. The present Town Library developed from a nucleus of about 20 printed books and 10 manuscripts bequeathed to the parish church by William Smart, draper and portman, by will dated 8 January 1598–9, for the use of the 'common preacher of the Town for the time being.' The collection was moved from the church to a separate building in 1612. See the article 'An ancient Public Library,' *Times Literary Supplement,* vol. 49 (1950), p. 524. Eight manuscripts of Smart's gift are described by M. R. James, 'Description of the Ancient Manuscripts in the Ipswich Public Library,' *Suffolk Institute of Archaeology,* vol. 22 (1936), pp. 86–102. The Benefactors' Book dates from 1615.

IRTHLINGBOROUGH, Northamptonshire. An S.P.C.K. library of 72 volumes was founded in 1710. Nothing of it now remains.

ISEL, Cumberland. None of the 16 books given in accordance with the will of Barnabas Oley, d. 1685 (see p. 19), now remain, but there is an original list of the books in the church safe, dated 1687.

KILDWICK, Yorkshire [*c.* 70]. Most of the books were given by Henry Currer of Kildwick Hall (? Henry Currer, d. 1723). The library is mentioned by T. D. Whitaker, *History of Craven,* 2nd ed. 1812, p. 165, and in *Notes and Queries,* 6th Series, vol. 6 (1882), p. 258.

KILMERSDON, Somerset. An S.P.C.K. library of 72 volumes was founded in 1711. A remnant existed in the time of Blades (*The Bookworm,* vol. 1 (1866), p. 158), but nothing now remains.

KING'S CLIFFE, Northamptonshire [*c.* 550]. A library founded by William Law in 1752 and maintained by the Governors of the Law and Hutcheson Charity. The books are kept in contemporary cupboards in a room of a house in the village. Over the door of the house is the inscription 'Books of Piety are here lent to any/Persons of this or yͤ Neighbouring Towns.' *A Catalogue of the Library at King's Cliffe,* drawn up by D. W. Barrett and C. Wordsworth, was printed in 1886, and re-edited in 1927. Many of the books are inscribed 'Belonging to the School at King's Cliffe,' with the date 1753.

KING'S LYNN, Norfolk [1880]. A library belonging to the Mayor and Corporation was founded in S. Margaret's Church in 1631. It was augmented in 1714 with 441 books valued at £160 bequeathed by Thomas Thurlin, rector of Gaywood, and at about the same time with 273 volumes given by Robert Barker, M.D., and with 387 volumes given by John Horn, master of the Grammar School. A still extant Benefactors' Book was given by John Arrowsmith, D.D., before 1641, when 319 volumes were listed in it. There are also 2 nineteenth-century catalogues. The books are now kept partly at the Public Library and partly at S. Nicholas's Church.

A library founded in S. Nicholas's Church in 1617 was later amalgamated with that at S. Margaret's.

See the excellent account by T. E. Maw, 'The Church Libraries of King's Lynn,' *The Antiquary,* vol. 40 (1904), pp. 235–40, with photographs of the old bookcases and of the frontispiece of the Benefactors' Book; also B. Mackerell, *History of King's Lynn,* 1738, pp. 86–8.

KING'S NORTON, Warwickshire [876]. The library was given to the parish by Thomas Hall, rector, ejected 1662, d. 1665. In Baxter MS. Treatises 9 in Dr. Williams's Library, Gordon Square, London, there are separate lists of the theological books 'given for a Library at Kingsnorton for the Use of the Minister of Kingsnorton, Mosely and Withal etc. and of the Two Schoolmasters there' and of 'Schoole bookes and Phylosophy given to Kings Norton Library.' The books were formerly housed in the Grammar School in the churchyard (for which see Pilgrim Trust, 20th Report (1950), pp. 21–2) and were transferred to the Reference Library of Birmingham Public Library on permanent loan in 1892. There is an early catalogue and also a typescript catalogue made in 1911. See W. S. Brassington in *Library Chronicle*, vol. 5 (1888), pp. 61–71.

KINGSBRIDGE, Devon [*c.* 300]. An S.P.C.K. library of 72 volumes was founded in 1711. There are now over 300 volumes in the library, but the only ten old volumes seem to be *Critici Sacri,* 9 vols., Amsterdam, 1698, and J. Walker, *Sufferings of the Clergy,* 1714. These were not among the books sent in 1711. A Kingsbridge library bookplate with the 'Tolle lege' inscription (see p. 33) is reproduced in *Journal of the Ex Libris Society,* vol. 12 (1903), p. 78.

KIRKOSWALD, Cumberland. An S.P.C.K. library of 66 volumes was founded in 1710. Nothing of it now remains.

LANGLEY MARISH, Buck-

inghamshire [*c.* 250]. A collection bequeathed by Sir John Kederminster of Langley Park, d. 1631, 'for the perpetual benefit of the vicar and curate of the parish of Langley, as for all other ministers and preachers of God's Word that would resort thither to make use of the books therein': see *Charity Commissioners,* 25th Report (1833), pp. 96–7, and also p. 99, where it is said that an ancient tablet in the Kederminster vault states that Sir John 'made and gave to this town for ever, the adjoining library, in 1623.' The library-room has elaborate and charming contemporary fittings: see E. C. Rouse, 'The Kederminster Library,' *Records of Bucks,* vol. 14 (1941–6), pp. 50–66. A catalogue on parchment, dated 1638, 'hangs in the library' (Rouse, p. 51). For illustrations, see pl. III of this publication.

LANTEGLOS - BY - CAMELFORD, Cornwall [over 209]. The library of Daniel Lombard, rector 1713–47, bequeathed to his successors in the rectory. About 120 volumes considered as worthless by the late bishop of Truro (the Rt. Revd. J. W. Hunkin) and 'an expert'* were burned about 1940. A list of the remainder (209 titles) has been supplied to the Central Council for the Care of Churches. The books are kept in the rectory.

LAWSHALL, Suffolk [121]. The books were mainly the gift of Stephen Camborne, rector, d. 1704, 'to my successors in the incumbency.' A list made in 1909 has been supplied to the Central Council for the Care of Churches. The books are kept in the rectory.

LEDSHAM, Yorkshire. Dr. Thomas Bray, d. 1730, bequeathed two boxes of books 'to the parish of Ledsham near Ferry Bridge,' probably at the instance of Lady Betty Hastings: cf. *Life of Bray*, p. 58.

LEICESTER, S. Martin. The present Town Library developed from a nucleus of books kept until 1632 in the church and apparently in the belfry of S. Martin's. This library is referred to in accounts for 1586–7, 1592–3 and 1593–4 when 'seven books were chaynedd in the Church': see T. North, *Accounts of the Churchwardens of Saint Martin's, Leicester*, 1884, pp. 132, 136–7. According to the incumbent writing in the 'Notitia Parochialis' no. 678 (see p. 22), Henry, Earl of Huntingdon, Lord President of York, d. 1595, gave several books which were placed in the church of S. Martin. This stock was increased by other benefactors, and in 1632 and 1633, upon the motion of John [Williams], then Lord Bishop of Lincoln, the corporation erected a 'convenient room at the west end of yᵉ Churchyard, in which the said books were placed, and considerable additions have been made to them by subsequent benefactors.' Lord Huntingdon's founding of the library is mentioned in the inscription on the posthumous portrait of him, commissioned about 1624, and now hung in the Mayor's Parlour at the Guildhall. It is reproduced, together with the inscription, in *Local Portraits*, a catalogue published by the Leicester Museums and Art Gallery in 1956.

LEWES, Sussex. Joseph Graves, rector of S. Peter and S. Mary Westout, bequeathed his library of 523 volumes in 1717 'in trust for the benefit of the inhabitants of the town of Lewes.' At the end of the century the remaining books were being 'left to moulder useless and unknown on a few shelves in the free school house in S. Anne's: such as were left were finally sold in 1823 for £53': see *History of Lewes*, 1795, pp. 266–7; T. W. Horsefield, *History of Lewes*, 1824, p. 315; *Charity Commissioners*, 30th Report (1837), p. 704.

LITTLE HARROWDEN, Northamptonshire. An S.P.C.K. library of 67 volumes was founded in 1711. Nothing of it now remains.

LIVERPOOL, S. Peter. John Fells, 'mariner,' gave £30 in 1715 to found a theological library. The books bought at this time and others added by later rectors numbered 217 in 1825 and 305 in 1893 when they were carefully catalogued by H. Peet in *An Inventory of the Plate . . . in the two Parish Churches of Liverpool, . . . together with a catalogue of the ancient Library in S. Peter's Church*, pp. 29–52 (cf. pp. vi, vii). The library was moved to the Diocesan Church House, South John Street, Liverpool, before 1903—it is listed in the catalogue of their library made in that year—and later became part of the Bishop Ryle Library there. This library was destroyed by enemy action in the last war. Many of the books were of the sixteenth and seventeenth centuries: see Christie, pp. 102–3.

LLANBADARN FAWR,

Cardiganshire. An S.P.C.K. library of 72 volumes was founded in 1710. The condition of the library in 1853 is described in *Notes and Queries*, vol. 8 (1853), p. 595, where it is said that 'many of the books were the gift of a Dr. Fowle, with his autograph, stating that they were given as a lending library to the parishioners.' No books remain.

L L A N R H O S (Eglws Rhôs), Caernarvonshire. An S.P.C. K. library of 72 volumes was founded in 1712. The original bookcase remains. According to information from the vicar of Doncaster in 1950, the books were thrown away by a curate in 1925.

L L A N T Y S I L I O, Denbighshire. An S.P.C.K. library was founded in 1720.

L O N D O N, S. Botolph, Aldgate. A collection of 330 books at S. Botolph, the church where Dr. Bray was rector 1708–30, is referred to in *Life of Bray*, p. 79. J. Maskell, in *Notes and Queries*, 6th Series, vol. 6 (1882), p. 258, says that Bray's library was kept in the vestry 'about twenty years ago.' In 1872 the S. Botolph 'Bray' library was transferred to Stratford, which figures in the list of libraries published by the Associates of Dr. Bray until 1912. Nothing is now known of the books at either Aldgate or Stratford.

L O N D O N, S. George the Martyr, Queen Square, Bloomsbury. The library (about 550 volumes, mainly of the seventeenth century) was sold by Puttick & Simpson, 30 May 1862, lots 577–688, 'by direction of the Churchwardens, and with the sanction of the Ecclesiastical Commissioners.' The church was founded in 1706. Robert Nelson and other members of S.P.C.K. were among the founders: see J. L. Miller, *History of the Church and Parish of S. George the Martyr*, 1881, where there is no mention of the library.

L O N D O N, S. Leonard, Shoreditch [c. 650]. In the vestry, south of the sanctuary, there was a library of 870 books, left by will of John Dawson of Hoxton Market Place, the shelves of which were inscribed, 'Oct. 14th, 1763, To the Vicar and Churchwardens of the Parish for the Time being and their successors for ever': see *Survey of London*, vol. 8 (1922), p. 102. 227 volumes were missing when the collection was moved to the Shoreditch Central Library in Pitfield Street, Hoxton. A catalogue compiled by William Burgess, parish clerk, was printed in J. Ware, *Account of the Charities of Shoreditch*, 1836, pp. 161–7. A full card-catalogue is being compiled.

L O N D O N, S. Martin-in-the-Fields. Archbishop Tenison founded a library in the churchyard of S. Martin-in-the-Fields in 1684, 'The bookes in the said library to be for public use, but especially for the use of the vicar and lecturer of the said parish, and of the said schoolmaster and usher for the time being, and the parsons of the parish churches of S. James's and S. Anne's, Westminster, and the King's chaplains in ordinary for the time being.' A catalogue of the books, *c.* 1700, is at Lambeth Palace Library. The 4,000 books were stated to be in 1849 'in as bad a state as books can be': see *Report from the Select Committee on Public Libraries,* 1849, pp. 64–9. They were dispersed in two sales by Leigh, Sotheby, & Wilkinson, 3 June 1861 (printed books, in 1,668 lots), and 1 July 1861 (manuscripts, in 98 lots). Manuscripts from this source are British Museum Add. 24191–202, 24663, 24666, 24686, 25033, 27278, 37785, 38914; Chicago University Library 409, Manchester, Rylands Lat. 227, and Eng. 82; Norwich Cathedral (Boccaccio); Paris, Bibl. Nat. nouv. acq. lat. 873; Harvard, Ital. 7; Washington, Folger 1809, 1. Sir Thomas Phillips acquired 29 lots (Phillipps MSS. 15730 –58). Samuel Ayscough's catalogue of the manuscripts made in 1786 is British Museum Add. MS. 11257. Lot 38 of the manuscripts was lot 2 in the Cockerell sale, April 1957, and lot 39, a collection of printed fragments, is in Cambridge University Library (ss. 3. 14).

LOSTWITHIEL, Cornwall [2]. An S.P.C.K. library of 72 volumes was founded in 1710. Two volumes remain, nos. 4, 10.

LOUGHBOROUGH, Leicestershire [*c.* 300]. James Bickham, rector, d. 1785, bequeathed a collection of books for the use of his successors. About 200 volumes are now kept in a room over the south porch, and 100 volumes are on deposit at the College of Further Education, Loughborough. G. D. Fletcher, *The Rectors of*

Loughborough, 1882, p. 34, refers to Bickham's request that four copies of a catalogue of the books should be made. No old catalogue is now known, but the books at Loughborough College have been listed.

LUDLOW, Shropshire. Two existing books contain an inscription recording that they belonged 'ad librariam ecclesie ludloiensis,' by gift of Richard Sparchford, archdeacon of Salop, in 1557. One, Appian, *Historia Romana,* Venice, 1477, was advertised for sale in W. & G. Foyle's catalogue for February 1957. The other, Picus Mirandula, *De Providentia Dei,* 1508, is Bodleian D. 2. 13 Art. Seld.

MAIDSTONE, Kent [*c.* 700]. A Walton's Polyglot was bought by the Corporation in 1658 and placed in the vestry for the use of ministers and others (Burghmote Records CC, ff. 94ᵛ, 96ᵛ). A list of 32 'Books in the Vestry Library, 24 June 1716' is in the Burial Register for 1678–1715. The collection was augmented in 1735 by the purchase for £50, raised by subscription, of a 'large and choice collection of books' from the library of Thomas Bray (J. M. Russell, *History of Maidstone,* 1881, pp. 121 –2), Maidstone having been the town which took advantage of the clause in Bray's will whereby all the historical, chronological, and geographical books in his library, as also the Fathers, the commentaries of Cornelius à Lapide and the works of Luther and Melanchthon, valued at £100, might be sold for £50 'towards the raising a Lending or Publick Library in any market town in England' (*Life of*

Bray, p. 59). A catalogue of these books, 238 folios, 129 quartos, and 192 octavos, etc., is in Bodleian MS. Rawlinson C. 155, ff. 286–92. The collection was moved from All Saints' Church to the Maidstone Museum in 1867. A *Catalogue of all the books in the Parochial Library of the Town and Parish of Maidstone,* by S. Weller, curate, was printed at the expense of John Lewis of Margate: it lists 681 volumes. A catalogue now at Maidstone was made by R. Finch in 1815 (724 volumes). See also S. W. Kershaw, 'On Manuscripts and Rare Books in the Maidstone Museum,' *Archaeologia Cantiana,* vol. 11 (1877), pp. 189–98.

MALDON, Essex [*c.* 5,000]. A collection bequeathed to his native town by Thomas Plume, d. 1704, and placed in a room erected by him over the school built on the site of S. Peter's Church, 'that any Gentleman or Scholar who desires may go into it' during the hours when the Library Keeper is in attendance, to read the books, or to borrow them against a 'Vadimonium.' The library was assisted by the Pilgrim Trustees in 1952 and 1955 (see the 22nd and 25th Reports of the Trust). A catalogue was made in 1848 and another is being prepared by S. G. Deed. The books in quarto and smaller sizes are described fully by Andrew Clark in Bodleian MSS. Eng. misc. c. 42–3. See also Clark in *Essex Review,* vol. 12 (1903), pp. 159–65, and *Charity Commissioners,* 32nd Report (1837–8), pp. 573–7. A copy of Plume's will is in Bodleian MS. Rawlinson, Essex 8, ff. 253–63.

MALTON, S. Leonard, Yorkshire. An S.P.C.K. library was founded in 1721. No books remain.

MANCHESTER. A library seems to have been begun in the Jesus Chapel of the Parish Church (now the Cathedral), c. 1640, soon after Henry Bury, by will in 1634, bequeathed £10 'to buy books with then to be payed when they shall have a convenient place of their owne furnished with bookes for the common use of the said parrish to the worth of a hundreth pounds': see Christie, pp. 5–8. In 1653 Humphrey Chetham bequeathed £200 'to be bestowed by my Executors in Godly English Books' such as they should 'think most proper for the edification of the common people' (Christie, p. 20), to be chained in the Parish Church (and in 4 other churches and chapels: see BOLTON; GORTON; TURTON; WALMESLEY). The 202 books bought for Manchester are listed in a schedule of 1665, printed by Christie, pp. 33–48. The chained library in the Jesus Chapel existed until about 1830, when the books were sold (Christie, p. 49). Some were then bought by James Crossley, President of the Chetham Society: for 5 of them, see G. J. French, *Bibliographical Notices of the Church Libraries at Turton and Gorton,* Chetham Society, vol. 38 (1855), pp. 184–95.

MARLBOROUGH, Wiltshire [*c.* 600]. Most of the books were bequeathed by William White, master of Magdalen College School 1632–48, and rector of Pusey, d. 1678, 'to

M

the Mayre and Corporation of Marl-
bourough in the County of Wilts for
the use of Mr Yate, Vicar of S. Maryes,
and of his successors for ever.' They
were transferred 'on permanent loan'
to Marlborough College in 1944. See
a full and interesting account of the
history of the library by E. G. H.
Kempston, 'The Vicar's Library,
S. Mary's, Marlborough,' *Wiltshire
Archaeological and Natural History
Magazine,* vol. 51 (1947), pp. 194–
215. Christopher Wordsworth compiled a catalogue in 1903.

MARSKE, Yorkshire. An S.P.C.K.
library of 72 volumes was founded in
1712. Nothing of it now remains.

MARTOCK, Somerset [13]. 13
volumes bequeathed by Richard
Busby, headmaster of Westminster
School, d. 1695, are now in the library
of Wells Cathedral. The bindings
bear Busby's arms. A list of the books
was sent to the Central Council for
the Care of Churches.

MENTMORE, Buckinghamshire
[*c.* 120]. About 200 volumes bequeathed (?) by William Beasley, rector of Cheddington 1716–42, d. 1743,
were deposited with the Bucks
Archaeological Society at Aylesbury,
in 1909. The more valuable of these
books were sold to Messrs. Blackwell
of Oxford *c.* 1940, and a few were
apparently destroyed at the same time.
The remainder became the property
of the Society. Many of the books
seem to have been acquired by Beasley when he was at King's College,
Cambridge (matric. 1697) and at
Eton.

MILDEN, Suffolk. William
Burkitt, rector 1678–1703, bequeathed
about 2,000 volumes to his successors.
Cf. *Notes and Queries,* 6th series,
vol. 7 (1883), p. 117. This library was
sold by A. F. Rivers, rector 1897–
1907, according to his successor in the
rectory (see *Proceedings of the Suffolk
Institute of Archaeology,* vol. 13
(1909), p. 238.

MILTON ABBAS, Dorset [7].
A wall-tablet in the Abbey church at
Milton Abbas commemorates the gift
of a library by John Tregonwell,
d. 1680, 'to the use of this abbey
church for ever. As a thankfull ac-
knowledgement of God's wonderfull
mercy in his preservation, when he
fell from the top of this church.' See
Canon J. M. J. Fletcher in *Proceedings of the Dorset Natural History
and Antiquarian Field Club,* vol. 35
(1914), p. 21; also *ibid.,* vol. 4, p. 87,
where it is said that the books numbered more than 60; also J. Hutchins,
History of Dorset, vol. 4, 1873,
pp. 407–8. The books, with 7 exceptions, were handed over for pulping
during the last war on a 'peremptory
order' * from the bishop. 'The order
was emphatically resisted by the
Vicar and Churchwardens, but in-
sisted upon by the authorities.' *

MONMOUTH. An S.P.C.K. library of 72 volumes was founded in
1710. Nothing of it now remains.

MORE, Shropshire [*c.* 250]. The
books were given by Richard More of
Linley in 1680 with the object of
'teaching the minister sound doctrine.'
They have been listed by R. Relton
and W. G. Clark-Maxwell in *Trans-*

actions of the Shropshire Archaeological Society, 3rd Series, vol. 7 (1907), pp. 117–24. A contemporary catalogue is noticed ibid., vol. 9 (1909), p. xxii (Miscellanea xv).

N A N T W I C H, Cheshire [165]. The collection formed c. 1704 (see J. Hall, History of Nantwich, 1883, pp. 301, 331) is 'in very poor condition.' * The books were mainly the gift of William Day 'for the use of ministers and other students.' The incumbent records in the 'Notitia Parochialis' of 1705 (see p. 22): 'A Library found and settling by yᵉ Clergy of this Deanery' (no. 1147). A catalogue dated in 1712 is kept in the rectory. A list of the books was sent to the Central Council for the Care of Churches. See also J. C. Cox, English Church Furniture, 1907, pp. 334–5; also, below, pl. IV (a).

N A Y L A N D, Suffolk [c. 100]. A list of 13 books printed in or before 1738 was sent to the Central Council for the Care of Churches. The rest are mainly nineteenth century.

N E W A R K - O N - T R E N T, Nottinghamshire [1,300]. Thomas White, vicar 1660–6, bishop of Peterborough, d. 1698, bequeathed 'to the Maior aldermen and vicar of the towne of Newarke upon Trent for the time being all my printed bookes to be a library, at least a good beginning of a Library, for the use of them and the inhabitants of that towne and the gentlemen and clergy of the adjacent countrey.' These books are in the parvise. A catalogue made in 1853 by W. Ridge was printed at Newark in 1854.

NEWCASTLE - UPON - TYNE, Northumberland [c. 300 + over 4,000]. A room known as the library existed at S. Nicholas's Church, now the Cathedral, as early as 1597. In the second half of the seventeenth century the books in the church seem to have been in the control of the Corporation, who appointed a salaried library-keeper in 1677. The incumbent records in the 'Notitia Parochialis' of 1705 (see p. 22), no. 1271: 'There is a little Library belonging to S.Nic. Church wᶜʰ was pillag'd by yᵉ Scots in yᵉ late Civil Wars. But since yᵉ Restoracion, Mʳ John Cosin Aldorman gave £80 towards yᵉ furnishing of it with books. Besides 20 volumes out of his own study wᶜʰ he left by his will to be made choice of by yᵉ vicar.' There were 300 volumes in 1721. Robert Thomlinson, rector of Whickham, gave about 1,600 volumes in 1735 and bequeathed a further 3,000 volumes in 1745 in trust for the library in S. Nicholas's Church. The Thomlinson books were transferred to the Newcastle Public Library in 1885. The 'Old Library' remains at S. Nicholas, except for one medieval manuscript (Richard Rolle's English Psalter) in the Public Library. A catalogue of the Thomlinson Collection and of the Old Library by E. Charnley was printed in 1829. A Catalogue of the Newcastle Chapter Library and of the Churchwardens' or Old Parish Library by E. B. Hicks and G. E. Richmond, printed in 1890, lists 298 volumes belonging to the Old Parish Library (pp. 32–46). See also B. Anderton in Book Auction Records, vol. 7 (1909–10), pp. vii–x; E. Mackenzie, Account of Newcastle upon Tyne, 1827, pp. 490–6.

NEWENT, Gloucestershire. John Craister, vicar, by will dated 1737, 'gave for ever, to the succeeding vicars of Newent, all his study of books' (*Charity Commissioners,* 18th Report (1828), p. 287). No books remain.

NEWPORT, Essex [*c.* 200]. An S.P.C.K. library of 72 volumes was founded in 1710. 49 of them remained in 1834 (see pp. 239–40 of the collection of catalogues of books sent out in 1817 and later years, belonging to the Associates of Dr. Bray), and 3 or 4 still remain. Of the present collection, 43 volumes are earlier than 1800. A list of these pre-1800 books has been sent to the Central Council for the Care of Churches.

NEWPORT, Monmouthshire [13]. An S.P.C.K. library of 72 volumes was founded in 1711. Nos. 5, 15, 16, 19, 20, 48, 51, 58, 60–2, 64 of these books, and probably some others are now in the Cathedral library at Llandaff.

NEWPORT PAGNELL, Buckinghamshire [3]. According to J. Staines, *History of Newport Pagnell,* 1842, Lewis Atterbury bequeathed books in 1731 (p. 133) and 'The Library at Newport Pagnell is in the custody of the Revd. George Morley, as the Master of Queen Anne's Hospital' (p. 134). The only books now at the church are Jewel, Foxe, and a Bible of 1608.

NEWQUAY, Cornwall [23]. A list of the books, all printed between 1622 and 1694, has been sent to the Central Council for the Care of Churches.

NORTH GRIMSTON, York-shire. Timothy Thurscross, archdeacon of Cleveland, d. 1671, directed in his will that his 'study of books' should be distributed to three Yorkshire churches 'for the vicars therein and their successors for ever.' According to J. Raine, *Catalogue of the printed books in the Library of the Dean and Chapter of York,* 1896, p. xiii, books from Thurscross's library bequeathed to North Grimston by Barnabas Oley, d. 1685, were there in 1731, 'but are now missing.' Cf. also the clause of Busby's will relating to Thurscross's books (G. F. R. Barker, *Memoir of Richard Busby,* 1895, pp. 142–3). The incumbent reported in the 'Notitia Parochialis' of 1705 (see p. 22), 'We have a very useful Library given and bequeath'd to the vicars for ever by . . . Timothy Thurscrosc' (no. 1008).

NORTH WALSHAM, Norfolk. An S.P.C.K. library of 67 volumes was founded in 1710. 63 of these books remained in 1870, together with about 85 other books of the sixteenth, seventeenth, and eighteenth centuries, and a few of later date. The collection seems to have remained intact at North Walsham until 1938, when the Secretary of the Associates of Dr. Bray suggested that 5 of the books should be sold to Messrs. Blackwell (they were sold in July) and that the others might as well be destroyed. None now remain, but the original 'Register' has been preserved, together with a catalogue made in 1870. A copy of this catalogue has been sent to the Central Council for the Care of Churches.

NORTHAMPTON, All Saints.

According to R. M. Serjeantson, *History of the Church of All Saints, Northampton,* 1901, p. 265, there was then a library in the upper vestry of the north transept, but there is not apparently any trace or memory of it now. It is referred to also in *Notes and Queries,* 6th Series, vol. 6 (1882), p. 15, where it is said that most of the books contained an inscription recording that they had been given by Dr. Crane, prebendary of Westminster, 'to the library of All Saints, in Northampton, MDCCLXXVII': a Pliny given in 1701, a Chaucer of 1542, and Walton's Polyglot are mentioned.

NORTON, Derbyshire [*c.* 390]. Nearly all the books, some of them now in bad condition, were bequeathed by Cavendish Nevile, rector 1710–49, d. 1749, and bear his bookplate. They are now on deposit in the Sheffield City Library.

NORTON - CUM - LENCH - WICK, Worcestershire [1]. Peter Cassy, vicar, d. 1784, bequeathed books for the use of his successors in the vicarage. They bore a printed label with the words 'For the Parochial Library of Norton & Lenchwick, by P. Cassy, Vicar,' and were kept in a room of the vicarage known as the Parish Room: see J. B. McGovern in *The Antiquary,* New Series, vol. 7 (1911), pp. 305–10, where the titles of 41 out of *c.* 360 volumes are given, and in *Notes and Queries,* vol. 154 (1928), p. 46; also *Notes and Queries,* 8th Series, vol. 7 (1895), pp. 241–3, where there is a list of the then missing books. The

collection was sold without authority in or shortly before 1951, and only one book, *The Clergy-man's Vade Mecum,* 1707, remains at Norton. 128 volumes from the library were offered for sale by Countryside Libraries Ltd., Hitchin, Herts, cat. no. 10 (1951), items 313–409. McGovern refers to a catalogue made by the Reverend H. W. Wood and to a printed list (8 leaves, octavo, no place or date of printing).

NORWICH. S. Andrew. 'In the south vestry are the remains probably of a parish library, among which a MS. of Trevisa's translation of the Epistles, Gospels, and most of the New Testament, in which is this 'Oh Deus Anselmi Barbour miserere Wylelmi' (*History of Norfolk,* 1829, vol. 2, p. 1178). No books remain.

NORWICH, S. Martin at Oak. 'In the vestry of this church are about 400 volumes of old books, given by the late rector, the Rev. Ephraim Meago' (*History of Norfolk,* 1829, vol. 2, p. 1237). No books remain.

NORWICH, S. Peter Mancroft [2]. Entries from the Churchwardens' Accounts mentioning the library in the church in 1629, 1647, and 1652 and a late-seventeenth-century catalogue of the books (90 volumes, nearly all in Latin), with names of donors, are printed by W. Rye, 'S. Peter Mancroft, Norwich: its Parish History in the Sixteenth and Seventeenth Centuries, with a Catalogue of the Books formerly given to and now in its Library,' *Norfolk Antiquarian Miscel-*

lany, vol. 2 (1883), pp. 345, 359–63. 'A booke to make a catalogue of yᵉ books in yᵉ Library' was bought in 1682. The two medieval manuscripts listed in the catalogue still remain (see p. 110), but none of the other books.

OAKHAM, Rutland [118]. The books were mainly given in 1616 by Anne, widow of John, 1st Baron Harington, of Exton, d. 1620, for the use of the vicar and benefit of the local clergy (cf. *Victoria County History,* vol. 2, p. 22).

OFFORD CLUNY, Huntingdonshire [17]. 'John Newcome D.D., rector 1730 to 1765 . . . left a legacy for the village school and a library of theological works for his successors in Offord Cluny': see T. Candlin, *Offord Cluny and Offord Darcy,* 1929, p. 24: for Newcome cf. GRANTHAM. The remaining volumes are marked 'Offord Cluny Library.' They have been recently moved into the church from a disused loft at Offord Darcy rectory where there were 'about 60' books in 1950. The Central Council has a list of the survivors.

OLDBURY, Shropshire. An S.P.C.K. library of 72 volumes was founded in 1713. Nothing of it now remains. See p. 35.

OTTERY ST. MARY, Devon [*c.* 250]. A library existed in 1672. 'In the gallery in the Lady Chapel, called the Library, are a few tattered remains of books. . . . Such books of value as still (1842) exist . . . are forthwith to be rebound and catalogued': see *An*

Account of the Church of Ottery S. Mary, Transactions of the Exeter Diocesan Architectural Society, vol. 1 (1842), pp. 40–1. 66 of the books now in the church are earlier than 1800.

OUNDLE, Northamptonshire. An S.P.C.K. library of 72 volumes was founded in 1711. Nothing of it now remains.

OVER WHITACRE, Warwickshire. An S.P.C.K. library of 72 volumes was founded in 1711. Nothing of it now remains.

OXENHALL, Gloucestershire. An S.P.C.K. library of 72 volumes was founded in 1710. Nothing of it now remains.

OXFORD, S. Peter-in-the-East [250]. The library was founded by W. K. Hamilton, vicar 1837–41 (bishop of Salisbury 1854–69), 15 August 1841. The date 1841 and the words 'E. LIBR. BIBL. S. PET. AD. OR. OXON.' are in gilt on the covers of all the books. 71 volumes are earlier than 1800. There is a manuscript catalogue and a register of loans 1841–76.

PERSHORE, Worcestershire. An S.P.C.K. library of 72 volumes was founded at Elmley in 1712 and transferred later to Pershore. Nothing of it now remains.

PLYMTREE, Devon [*c.* 300]. The books are said to be mainly the bequest of John Fleming, rector 1778 –96. They are kept in the rectory.*

POULTON-LE-FYLDE, Lancashire [71]. An S.P.C.K. library

was founded in 1720, apparently of 81 volumes and identical with that sent to WHITCHURCH, Hants (q.v.). 71 volumes, nos. 1–8, 10, 11, 13, 15–26, 28, 30–62, 64–71, 73, 75–80 of the books recorded in the Whitchurch catalogue, remain at Poulton. The library is noticed as a 'complete and excellently preserved Bray library' by Christie, p. vi.

PREES, Shropshire [c. 300]. The books, mostly earlier than 1800, were bequeathed for the use of the vicars of Prees for ever by John Allen, vicar 1846–83, and contain a book-plate to this effect. They were kept at the vicarage, but have recently been transferred as a gift to the County Record Office, Shirehall, Shrewsbury. A list of the books has been sent to the Central Council for the Care of Churches.

PRENDERGAST, Pembrokeshire. An S.P.C.K. library of 72 volumes was founded in 1710. Nothing of it now remains.

PRESTON-BY-WINGHAM, Kent [41]. An S.P.C.K. library of 67 volumes was founded in 1710. The original cupboard remains, together with nearly all the books, except those in the top shelf (nos. 1–24, 26–35, 38–42, 45–6). No. 9 is the Register. 'The Catalogue of Preston Library April ye 16th 1730. Then Exhibited by the Vicar at the Visitation' is in Canterbury Cathedral MS. Y. 4. 30, pp. 133–9.

PWLLHELI, Caernarvonshire. An S.P.C.K. library of 67 volumes was

founded in 1712. With the consent of the minister, this library was amalgamated in 1770 with a lending library of 260 volumes then sent by the Associates of Dr. Bray. Nothing of it now remains.

REEPHAM, Norfolk. For the sale of books marked 'Reepham Church Library,' c. 1843, see Notes and Queries, 1st Series, vol. 7 (1853), p. 392.

REIGATE, Surrey [c. 2,000]. The library was begun in 1701 by Andrew Cranston, vicar 1697–1708, and was confirmed by a deed of foundation, 4 November 1708, as a public library 'for the use and perusal of the Freeholders Vicar and Inhabitants': see W. Hooper, Reigate, 1945, pp. 62–7, and G. Smith in the Library Association Record, vol. 12 (1910), p. 254. The Benefactors' Book, instituted in 1701, shows that nearly all the books were given by numerous donors soon after this date. Cranston wrote in the 'Notitia Parochialis' of 1705 (see p. 22), no. 535 : 'There are at present about 1,600 volumes great and small. And the library is daily encreasing.' An inaccurate catalogue was printed in 1893 : Bibliotheca Reigatiana, Catalogue of the Public Library at Reigate. The Pilgrim Trust contributed £500 towards the repair of the library-room above the vestry and the books in 1951 (see 21st Report, pp. 43–4) and £50 per annum is contributed by the Surrey County Council. W. Hooper's Guide to Reigate Church, 3rd ed. 1951, contains a photograph of the library.

RIBCHESTER, Lancashire

[1]. In 1684 Bradley Hayhurst, incumbent of Macclesfield, left his library 'to the Parish Church of Ribchester . . . where I was born.' Only 6 volumes remained at the end of the nineteenth century and only 1 now remains: see *The Antiquary*, vol. 23 (1891), pp. 4, 21–2, 139, and Christie, pp. 104–5. Ralph Thoresby visited the library above the north porch in 1702 (*Diary*, vol. 1, p. 391).

R I V I N G T O N , Lancashire. Christie, p. 106, records that 14 books are listed in an eighteenth-century minute-book belonging to the church and that 4 of these books were in existence in 1856. None now remains.

R O T H E R H A M , Yorkshire. After the death of Edward Mansel in 1704, his widow, Frances, gave 'a library, chiefly of theological works, to the amount of £100, for the use of the clergy and parishioners of Rotherham for ever': see J. Eastwood, *History of Ecclesfield*, 1862, p. 202. Nothing is now known of these books.

R O U G H A M , Norfolk. Books belonging to Roger North, d. 1734, and to his niece Dudleya North, d. 1712, were formed into a parochial library in 1714 and kept in a room attached to the north aisle of the church 'for the use of the minister . . . and under certain regulations and restrictions, of the neighbouring clergy also, for ever': see G. Ballard, *Memoirs of Several Ladies*, 1752, p. 415. A catalogue on parchment among episcopal records at Norwich is headed 'Anno Salutis MDCCXIIII Catalogus Bibliothecae Ecclesiae Rougham,' and lists

about 1,150 volumes. Anne North bequeathed £20 to the library: the receipt for this sum, dated 22 April 1722, is Bodleian MS. North b. 17, f. 94. See A. Jessopp, *Lives of the Norths*, vol. 3, 1890, pp. 261, 303, 309.

R O Y S T O N , Hertfordshire. 'In the old vestry room under the tower is a library of some two hundred books, presented for the most part by Leonard Chappelow, vicar from 1731 to 1739,' and professor of Arabic at Cambridge from 1720 until his death in 1768 (A. Kingston, *History of Royston*, 1906, p. 96). 30 volumes from this library were listed in catalogue 13 (1953) of the Cambridge bookseller R. C. Pearson, and 9 others were bought from Pearson by the Bodleian (one bearing Chappelow's name is Vet a. 2 f. 135). In addition, a collection of 'about thirty old books,' * found during the restoration of the tower roof, was sold 'for £10 to a then parishioner.' * No faculty was applied for for these sales.

S T . B E E S , Cumberland. An S.P.C.K. library of 66 volumes was founded in 1712. Nothing of it now remains.

S T . M A R T I N , Shropshire. An S.P.C.K. library was founded in 1721.

S T . N E O T S , Huntingdonshire [*c.* 90]. The collection consists of 50 volumes of the S.P.C.K. library of 72 volumes founded in 1711, together with about 40 other volumes, mainly works of the protestant reformers, given by William Cole, rector of

Eynesbury, d. 1783. Nos. 2–7, 10–20, 26, 28–9, 31–2, 34–48, 50–3, 55–6, 58–60, 63, 65–7 of the S.P.C.K. library remain. A list of the books was sent to the Central Council for the Care of Churches.

SALFORD, Sacred Trinity, Lancashire [62]. Humphrey Oldfield, d. 1690, bequeathed his divinity books. The collection consisted of 72 volumes when it was presented by the rector and vestry to the Salford Central Library in 1876. There are now 62 volumes, a list of which has been sent to the Central Council for the Care of Churches. See Christie, pp. 107–8.

SHEFFIELD, Yorkshire. The incumbent records in the 'Notitia Parochialis' of 1705 (see p. 22), no. 1014: 'A place for a library is fitted up in yᵉ vestry of yᵉ Church and a small Collection of Books made.'

SHELDON, Warwickshire [over 300]. A library was 'founded by the present incumbent' [i.e. Thomas Bray, rector 1690–1729, d. 1730] and was placed 'in a large room over the Charity School and vestry' built by the patron Lord Digby, according to the return in the 'Notitia Parochialis' of 1705 (see p. 22), no. 213. Bray left 'my Library at Sheldon . . . To and for the sole use of the Incumbent thereof for the time being and his Successors for ever.' He also left the residue of his books not otherwise bequeathed 'to be divided, at the discretion of Mr. Samuel Smith, to the Parochial Library of Sheldon, and to Professor Hamilton of Edinburgh, for the purpose of distributing them to

the Lending Libraries in the Highlands of Scotland' (*Life of Bray,* p. 59). A list of some of the books, *c.* 80 titles, was sent to the Central Council for the Care of Churches.

SHEPSHED, Leicestershire. An S.P.C.K. library valued at £23 9s. 3d. was founded in 1720. No books remain.

SHIPDHAM, Norfolk [490]. The collection, 1,344 volumes, is believed to have been largely the library of Thomas Townsend, rector 1707–54, d. 1764, bequeathed 'to his successors for ever.' Many books contain the name of Peter Needham (d. 1731: see *Dict. Nat. Biogr.*). 852 volumes were sold at Hodgson's, 29 March 1951, in 220 lots: for 31 of these see R. C. Pearson's catalogue 11, nos. 420–47, 467, 757. The 490 volumes excluded from the sale are now in the Norwich Central Library. Two medieval manuscripts were sold separately to Cambridge University Library and are now Add. MSS. 7220, 7221. In *Notes and Queries,* 2nd Series, vol. 12 (1861), p. 469, Blades recounts his visit to Shipdham in search of Caxtons (which he did not find). See also *The Times,* 7 November 1927, pp. 15, 17; G. A. Stephen, *A Norfolk Bibliography,* 1921, pp. 42–4.

SHIPLAKE, Oxfordshire. A typescript inventory in the Bodleian Library records a library catalogue of 1661 among parish records. No books remain.

SHUSTOKE, Warwickshire. An S.P.C.K. library was founded in

97

1727: see the Minutes of the Library Committee 1705–1730 in archives of S.P.C.K., p. 159 (meeting of 7 April 1727). No books remain.

SIBLE HEDINGHAM, Essex. Moses Cook, rector 1690–1733, d. 1733, bequeathed a library, which was kept in the rectory and was sold with the effects of the rector in 1918 (information from the dean of Gloucester in 1957).

SKELTON (near Guisborough), Yorkshire. An S.P.C.K. library was founded in 1720. Nothing of it now remains.

SKIPTON, Yorkshire [c. 1,700]. Sylvester Petyt, principal of Barnard's Inn, d. 1719, founded the library with gifts of books before 1708 and at various dates after 1708. In the 'Notitia Parochialis' of 1705 (see p. 22) the incumbent notes that 'a library of indifferent value is setling by Silvester Pettite Esqr of Barnard's Inn' (no. 856). Later about 60 books were given by Christopher Bateman, bookseller of Paternoster Row, and about 100 books by William Busfeild of the Inner Temple. The collection was moved from the vestry of the church to the Skipton Public Library in 1881. See W. H. Dawson, *History of Skipton*, 1882, pp. 346–50. Dawson mentions a volume of original catalogues kept with the books.

SLAITHWAITE, Yorkshire [25]. Robert Meeke, minister of Slaithwaite chapel, bequeathed books for the minister of the parish in 1724. According to W. Blades in *The Book-worm*, vol. 1 (1866), p. 173, they numbered about 150 volumes, but only 25 volumes now remain. A list has been sent to the Central Council for the Care of Churches.

SLAPTON, Devon. An S.P.C.K. library of 72 volumes was founded in 1710. Nothing of it now remains.

SLEAFORD, Lincolnshire [20]. 'There is a library fixing in ye Parish Mr. Edward Smith having given some Books towards it, who was ye Late Vicar,' according to the return in the 'Notitia Parochialis' of 1705 (see p. 22), no. 28. Smith was vicar from 1691 to 1703. The books, mainly of the later seventeenth century, and all in English, were chained to a reading-desk, but have now been moved to a modern bookcase. They are listed by E. Trollope, *Sleaford*, 1872, pp. 165–6, and mentioned by Streeter, p. 290.

SOUTHAMPTON, S. Michael. A cupboard in the church bears the inscription 'John, sonne of John Clungeon of this town, Alderman, erected this Presse and gave certain books, who dyed anno 1646.' The cupboard, which is of some size, is now empty of books. The four chained books now in the church are not likely to have been part of this library.

SPALDING, Lincolnshire [c. 600]. The library was begun in the room over the church porch in 1637 for the use of the minister and his successors for ever, 'Yet so that any one of the Town who had given any books to the Librarie should with his consent have libertie to borrow what books they pleased,' according to the testimony of William Sneath, aged 68, in 1661. This 'Parochial Library' was added to by the Spalding Gentlemen's Society in the early eighteenth century and was transferred by their efforts to the vestry. The collection, 'upwards of 600 volumes,' was moved to the Grammar School in 1865, when the church was rebuilt. It is said to be now the property of the Gentlemen's Society, and is housed in their rooms. See the *South Holland Magazine*, vol. 2 (1870), pp. 57–9, and E. M. Sympson, *Memorials of Old Lincolnshire*, 1911, pp. 320, 322, 337. Most of the books have 'Spalding' on the fore-edge. The Gentlemen's Society possesses 2 catalogues compiled by their members in the second decade of the eighteenth century: the names of the donors are here recorded.

STAINTON, near Guisborough, Yorkshire [*c.* 300]. The incumbent records in the 'Notitia Parochialis' of 1705 (see p. 22), no. 1058: 'My immediate predecessor Mr Richard Lumley A.M. bequeathed his Library for ever to ye use of the Minister or Curate for ye time being or whether of them resident there.' Lumley died in 1694. Most of the books bear his name and many of them also the name of William Lawson in a sixteenth-century hand. The books were transferred from the vicarage to York Minster Library after 1896 and before 1939. A note on the collection by Miss E. Brunskill is in the *Report of the Friends of York Minster*, 1947.

STAMFORD, S. Mary, Lincolnshire [*c.* 150]. Richard Banister,

d. 1626, gave books in his lifetime and prepared a place for them in the chancel. He also bequeathed £10 to the minister and churchwardens to be laid out at 7 per cent and the interest 'bestowed uppon divinity-bookes yearely or once in two yeares: and the same bookes shall bee placed in the Library in the said Church there to remaine for ever': see A. Sorsby, 'Richard Banister and English Opthalmology,' *Science, Medicine and History: Essays in Honour of Charles Singer*, vol. 2, 1953, p. 50. A catalogue-book given by Banister records purchases from 1633 to 1641 (pp. 17–18), and contains a list of books made in 1720. The books in the library bear dates between 1506 and 1748. They contain a label inscribed 'This Book belongs to the Library in *S. Mary's Church* in *Stamford*, Lincolnshire.' A list of them, made in 1928, has been sent to the Central Council for the Care of Churches.

STANGROUND, Huntingdonshire. A tablet in the north aisle records that William Whitehead, rector, d. 1755, bequeathed his library 'in usum successorum' appointing the rectors of Woodston and Fletton as trustees 'ut integra semper descendat': see W. D. Sweeting, *Parish Churches in and around Peterborough*, 1868, p. 196. According to Sweeting there were 1,000 volumes. The rector informed the Central Council in 1950 that he had 'sold the Library for £90 some years ago; after permission from all concerned.'

STANSTED MOUNT-FITCHET, Essex. 15 books 'belonging to the vestry' are listed in tithe accounts 1712–54 (Essex Record Office, D/P 109/3/2), one being *Paradise Lost*. The titles of 4 seventeenth-century books in the church library are recorded in a note-book of the later nineteenth century (T/P 68/25/3).

STEEPLE ASHTON, Wiltshire [*c.* 250]. The collection at the vicarage consists of 5 volumes of Chrysostom bequeathed by Ellis Wright, vicar 1538–69 (see *Wiltshire Notes and Queries,* vol. 6 (1910), p. 371), and about 250 volumes bequeathed by Samuel Hey, vicar 1787 –1828. A manuscript Book of Hours is described by C. Wordsworth, 'Horae Eboracenses,' *Surtees Society,* vol. 132 (1920), p. 161. A 'considerable number of books of sermons of the early 19th and late 18th centuries were discarded for salvage' * during the last war.

STOCKTON-ON-TEES, Co. Durham. In 1847 there were about 800 volumes. 204 of these, chiefly in Latin, had been left for the use of the church by John Stock, schoolmaster (son of Robert Stock, parish clerk, d. 1719). The others belonged to a subscription library started in 1800 by John Brewster, vicar 1799 –1805. See T. Richmond, *Local Records of Stockton and the Neighbourhood,* 1868, pp. 58, 99.

STOKE-BY-NAYLAND, Suffolk [*c.* 116]. C. M. Torlesse, *Some account of Stoke by Nayland,* 1877, prints on pp. 97–9 a bare list of 116 volumes under the heading 'Catalogue of the books called the Stoke Library kept in the room over the South Porch of the Church. The greater part, if not the whole of these, was given by the Rev. Thomas Reeve, vicar from 1685–1719.' See also H. M. Cautley, *Suffolk Churches,* 1927, p. 318.

STONEHOUSE, Gloucestershire [786]. Samson Harris, vicar, d. 1763, left his books 'unto the churchwardens of the parish of Stonehouse for the time being upon trust,' to be applied in accordance with the Act of 7 Anne (cf. R. Bigland, *Gloucestershire,* Supplement, pt. 4, under Stonehouse). These books and others—some belonged to J. Hilton, vicar 1708–23—were in process of being transferred from the church to the Secondary Modern School, on deposit in 1958. A full catalogue compiled by H. E. Hawkins in 1930–2 is kept at the vicarage.

STOWEY, Somersetshire. An S.P.C.K. library was founded in 1720.

SUDBURY, All Saints, Suffolk. An S.P.C.K. library of 67 volumes was founded in 1712 and 5 volumes of Bishop Patrick's works were added to it in 1750: see C. Badham, *All Saints Church, Sudbury,* 1852, pp. 105–9. Nothing of it now remains.

SUTTON COURTENAY, Berkshire [24]. Books were given in 1686, 1702, 1709, 1710 and other years. All but two have been chained. The bindings of 13 were repaired or renewed by John Gregson, vicar, in 1847. A list of the books has been made for the Central Council for the Care of Churches: all of them are in English.

SWAFFHAM, Norfolk [c. 400]. The books are supposedly a bequest from a member of the family of Spelman of Narborough in 1622. Some of them belonged in the later sixteenth century to Thomas Freake and Thomas Thetford: for persons of these names cf. J. A. Venn, *Alumni Cantabr.*, pt. 1 (1922–7). See *Notes and Queries*, vol. 7 (1853), p. 438; G. A. Stephen, *A Norfolk Bibliography*, 1921, p. 44; F. Blomefield, *History of Norfolk*, vol. 6, 1807, p. 217. A book-plate of the Swaffham library dated 1737, 'F. Dalton, F. Rayner, churchwardens,' is in the Franks Collection of Book-plates in the British Museum (no. 33865).

SWINDERBY, Lincolnshire. A list of 108 volumes, headed 'A Catalogue of Books belonging to the Parish of Swinderby,' is at the end of Parish Register II (1677–1802) now deposited with the Lincolnshire Archives Committee. Of these, 73 volumes were bequeathed by the Revd. Samuel Disney, lecturer at Wakefield, d. 1741, 'as a parochial library for ever,' 29 volumes were bequeathed by A. Chambers, vicar, in 1821, and 6 (the 6 volumes of Walton's Polyglot) by John Drake, vicar. A copy of the list has been sent to the Central Council for the Care of Churches. No books remain.

TADCASTER, Yorkshire. An S.P.C.K. library of 67 volumes was founded in 1710. Nothing of it now remains.

TANKERSLEY, Yorkshire [32]. Robert Booth, by will proved 10 January 1615, bequeathed books to John Nevinson, rector, d. 1634, and his successors for ever. 32 books formerly at Tankersley were recovered by A. W. Douglas, rector, in 1947 'from the cock-loft' * of Worsborough vicarage. They were transferred to York Minster Library after 1951. A list of them has been sent to the Central Council for the Care of Churches.

THURNHAM, Kent. An inventory of church goods taken at Easter 1751 lists about 130 books under the heading 'A Book Case Containing the Following Books.' The inventory is preserved in the Kent County Archives Office, Maidstone: see Felix Hull, *Guide to the Kent County Archives Office*, 1958, p. 118.

THURSBY, Cumberland. 14 of the 16 books sent to Thursby in accordance with the will of Barnabas Oley, d. 1685 (see p. 19) are listed in a church Terrier of 1830. None now remain there.

TIDEFORD, Cornwall. 30 to 40 old calf-bound volumes of eighteenth-century Theology were an heirloom at the vicarage, but disappeared fairly recently (information from Canon J. H. Adams, rector of Landulph).

TINSLEY, Yorkshire. An S.P.C.K. library of 72 volumes was founded in 1711. Nothing of it now remains, but the existence of 66 volumes was reported to the Associates of Dr. Bray in 1877. One volume (no. 69,

Herbert) with the Tinsley book-plate (see p. 34) is in the Department of Prints and Drawings in the British Museum.

TIVERTON, Devon [over 300]. John Newte, rector, d. 1715, bequeathed 250 volumes towards 'a Parochial Library . . . to be for ever kept in the chamber over the vestry in the Parish Church of Tiverton for the use of several Rectors and Curates thereof and of the School Masters of Mr. Blundel's Grammar School and Mr. Chilcot's English School for the time being.' There are now about 300 volumes earlier than 1715. A 'Catalogue of the Vestry Library' was printed by E. S. Chalk, *A History of the Church of S. Peter, Tiverton*, Tiverton, 1905, App., pp. xxv–lviii: see also pp. 71–3 for a description of the library and pp. 73–6 for a full account of the fifteenth-century manuscript Book of Hours belonging to the church.

TONG, Shropshire [over 400]. The library was founded by Gervase, Lord Pierrepont, in 1697 'for the use of the minister and his successors' and was increased by 91 volumes bequeathed by Lewis Peitier, vicar, d. 1745, 'to make part of it for ever.' It is kept in 4 spacious contemporary cupboards. The former contents of each cupboard are listed on paper sheets inside the doors. There is a contemporary catalogue on parchment, a copy of which was given to the Shrewsbury Free Library by the Revd. J. E. Auden. An inaccurate catalogue by Beriah Botfield is printed in the *Miscellanies of the Philobiblon*

Society, vol. 3 (1856–7), pp. 17–42. See also J. E. Auden, 'The Minister's Library in Tong Church,' *Transactions of the Shropshire Archaeological Society*, 4th Series, vol. 12 (1930), pp. 48–60; G. Griffiths, *History of Tong*, 1894, pp. 96, 107; *Charity Commissioners*, 3rd Report (1820), p. 259.

TORTWORTH, Gloucestershire [c. 650]. A library was bequeathed by Henry Brooke, rector, d. 1757 (for whom see *Dict. Nat. Biogr.*). About 650 volumes remain at the rectory. Others are believed to have been sold with the Tortworth Court (Ducie) library in 1949.*

TOTNES, Devon [c. 300]. The seventeenth-century gift-book belonging to the Corporation of Totnes (cf. *Charity Commissioners*, 7th Report (1822), pp. 50 *seq.*) records that Gabriel Barber gave £10 in 1619 'towards procuring a library,' and refers to bequests of books and money for books in 1620 and later. The library is referred to as 'publique' in 1634. Notices of the library, not recording its history, are in *Notes and Queries*, vol. 7 (1853), p. 463 (and thence in *Transactions of the Devonshire Association*, vol. 8 (1876), p. 772) and in *Devon and Cornwall Notes and Queries*, vol. 20 (1939), p. 224. A catalogue printed by C. Worthy, *Ashburton and its Neighbourhood*, 1875, pp. xxvii–xxxiii, lists 334 volumes, all but one of which were printed before 1670.

TREVETHIN, Monmouth. An S.P.C.K. library of 72 volumes was

founded in 1711. The Register only remains: see V. W. T. Rees, *Trevethin, Pontypool*, 1934, p. 62.

TURTON, Lancashire [51]. 71 volumes were bought with money bequeathed by Humphrey Chetham, d. 1653 (see MANCHESTER) and listed in a schedule of 1659 printed by Christie, pp. 57–9. 40 of these volumes remain, together with 11 volumes which seem to have been intended originally for WALMESLEY (q.v.). An annotated catalogue of them by G. J. French is in *Bibliographical Notices of the Church Libraries at Turton and Gorton,* Chetham Society, vol. 38 (1855), pp. 10–103. The books were repaired and rechained in their original cupboard in 1855: for their condition previously see *ibid.,* pp. 5–8. See also Streeter, pp. 304–6, with a photograph of the cupboard, and Blades, pp. 41–3 and Appendix B (pp. 61–2), where a catalogue is printed.

WALMESLEY, Lancashire. Probably the 25 books designed for Walmesley in accordance with the will of Humphrey Chetham, d. 1653, were diverted to TURTON (q.v.): see Christie, pp. 59–60 for a list of the books made in 1659 and printed by him. 11 of them are now at Turton.

WARWICK, S. Mary [1,383, including pamphlets in bound volumes]. A library 'for the use of Theological Readers in Warwick and its Neighbourhood' was founded in 1701 and a Benefactors' Book was begun in the same year (cf. REIGATE). The in-cumbent reported in the 'Notitia Parochialis' of 1705 (see p. 22), no. 627: 'We are about setling a Library, having had encouragement from Dr Bray of Sheldon in this County, Dr Maynard of Boddington in Northamptonshire, and ye contributions of some of ye neighbouring Clergy: The Lord Brook, Ld. Guilford, Ld. Digby, Lady Bowyer and others have been Benefactors to it.' See W. T. Carter in the *Journal of the British Archaeological Association,* New Series, vol. 16 (1910), pp. 53–61 (with a photograph of the library-room); *The Times,* 19 October 1956; *The Times Literary Supplement,* 1957, p. 40; P. Morgan and E. H. Painter in *The Library,* 5th Series, vol. 12 (1957), pp. 225–7. A catalogue in manuscript compiled in 1709 is among the parish records. A catalogue by the Revd. A. C. Irvine was printed in 1881 'for the use of the subscribers to the library,' and a catalogue by W. T. Carter was printed privately in 1910. A full catalogue by Paul Morgan of Birmingham University Library is in typescript. The Benefactors' Book and the pre-1800 books (numbering 965) are at present housed in the Warwick County Record Office. See also above, p. 59.

WENDLEBURY, Oxfordshire. 55 volumes, mainly seventeenth-century editions of the Greek and Latin Fathers, were bequeathed by Robert Welborne, rector 1730–64, as a parochial library. A note-book preserved at the church contains Welborne's own list of these books and his directions as to their future custody, with an extract from the Act of 7 Anne.

Two of the directions are that money given for augmenting the library should be spent on completing the collection of the works of the Fathers of the six first centuries, and that no book in any modern language should be admitted. An added note records that in 1840 the volumes were repaired and many of them rebound and all marked WENDLEBURY in gilt on the covers, at the expense of Jacob Ley, Censor of Christ Church. In spite of this, they 'had become so musty and decayed that they were destroyed some years ago' (information from the vicar in 1950). A copy of the list of books and of the other notes about them was sent to the Central Council for the Care of Churches.

WENTNOR, Shropshire [108]. Most of the books were bequeathed by Edward Rogers, rector of Myndtown, d. 1788. See 'The Library of Wentnor Church,' *Transactions of the Shropshire Archaeological Society*, vol. 46 (1931–2), p. i (Miscellanea I).

WENTWORTH, Yorkshire. An S.P.C.K. library of 67 volumes was founded in 1711. Nothing of it now remains.

WEOBLEY, Herefordshire. An S.P.C.K. library of 67 volumes was founded in 1710. Nothing of it now remains.

WESTERHAM, Kent. Charles West gave several hundred volumes in 1765. In 1856 the books had gone, but there was a catalogue of them in the parish chest (but not, it seems, now): see *Notes and Queries,* 2nd Series, vol. 2 (1856), p. 78.

WHITCHURCH, Hampshire [2]. An S.P.C.K. library of 81 volumes was founded in 1720. The monument in the church to Joseph Wood, vicar, d. 1731, records that he 'left a handsome library of books for the use of his successors.' About 660 volumes were sold at Sotheby's, 7 November 1927, lots 1–176, 'at the Request of the Vicar and Parochial Church Council and by permission of the Chancellor of the Diocese': the sale catalogue describes 329 printed items and 16 manuscripts, one of them medieval (lot 4). Lots 9, 29, 64 went to the British Museum and 166 volumes in 45 lots to Sir Leicester Harmsworth.

A volume in the Edward Edwards collection in the Manchester Central Library contains: (*a*) a printed catalogue of the S.P.C.K. library (another copy is Bodleian Rawlinson D. 834 f. 31); (*b*) 'A Catalogue of the Parochial Library (exclusive of those Books in the Press) at Whitchurch in Hampshire, August 30th, 1730'; this lists 587 volumes, and omits the S.P.C.K. library; (*c*) a full catalogue made by Edward Edwards in 1850 of 1,193 titles, including all the pamphlets, but excluding the manuscripts. Edwards's catalogue lists some items which do not appear to have been sold in 1927, e.g. Lyly, *Euphues* (1607), Works of Sir Thomas More (1557), Augustine, *Meditationes* (1502). The writer of a letter to the Central Council in 1950 referred to some of these books as having been at Whitchurch in 1912. He also said that a number of the earlier books in the library had belonged to Richard Brook (d. 1593, and buried at Whitchurch).

For the condition of the library in 1849 and in 1867, see *Report from the Select Committee on Public Libraries*, 1849, p. 25, and E. Edwards, *Free Town Libraries*, 1869, pp. 9–11. A manuscript given by Wood was published by Walter Money, *A Purveyance of the Royal Household in Elizabethan Times*, 1901. This manuscript, the Second Prayer Book of Edward VI (1552), and a copy of Edwards's catalogue made in 1901 are still at Whitchurch. See also *The Times*, 13 October 1927, p. 12.

W H I T C H U R C H, Shropshire [over 1,000]. The collection kept in the rectory consists partly of the books of Clement Sankey, rector, bought by Jane, Dowager Countess of Bridgewater, in 1707 for £305 and given by her in 1717, and partly of books bequeathed by Francis Henry, 8th Earl of Bridgewater, rector 1770–1829. According to a writer in *Notes and Queries*, vol. 8 (1853), p. 570, the number of volumes given in 1717 was 2,250, and according to the *Report from the Select Committee on Public Libraries*, 1849, p. 225, there were then 3,077 volumes.

W I G T O N, Cumberland. 16 volumes were sent in accordance with the will of Barnabas Oley, d. 1685 (see p. 19), and an S.P.C.K. library of 67 volumes was sent in 1710. No books remain, but according to J. Nicolson and R. Burn, *History of Westmorland and Cumberland*, 1777, vol. 2, p. 195, there was a 'pretty large parochial library.'

W I L L E N, Buckinghamshire. Richard Busby, headmaster of Westminster School, d. 1695, bequeathed part of his books 'for the use of the Ministry to be placed in the library belonging to the Church at Willen ... built ... by me at my own great charge' (cf. G. F. R. Barker, *Memoir of Richard Busby*, 1895, p. 142). In the catalogue of Busby's books at Westminster School 148 titles are marked 'Willen.' Other books were bequeathed by James Hume, rector of Bradwell, Bucks, d. 1734. The library, 619 volumes, was moved from the church to the vicarage before 1895 and was destroyed there by fire, 1 May 1946. A *Catalogue of Books in the Library at Willen* (preface signed by George Phillimore, vicar) was printed at Newport Pagnell in 1848: copies belong to Westminster School and to the Trustees of Dr. Busby's Charity, Dean's Yard, Westminster Abbey.

W I M B O R N E, Dorset [*c.* 240]. A chained library was founded with a bequest from William Stone, vicar, d. 1685, and was added to largely by gifts from Roger Gillingham, d. 1695, from Thomas Anstey, vicar, in 1697, and from Samuel Conant, d. 1719. For its history, see Blades, pp. 5–13, and in *The Library*, vol. 1 (1889), pp. 413–15; Canon J. M. J. Fletcher in *Proceedings of the Dorset Natural History and Antiquarian Field Club*, vol. 35 (1914), pp. 25–6; Streeter, pp. 295–7 (with a photograph); J. Hutchins, *History of Dorset*, vol. 3, 1868, p. 204. A catalogue was printed by Blades, pp. 14–19, and there are earlier catalogues in print (1863) and in manuscript (1725). The books were taken great care of by Canon Fletcher (vicar 1906–19) and are in excellent condition. See pl. IV (*b*).

WISBECH, Cambridgeshire [?]. 'About the time of the Restoration the Ten *Capital Burgesses* of the Town of Wisbech . . . prepared the Chamber over the Church-Porch, with Shelves and other Necessaries, for the Reception of Books. And several other Gentlemen at the same time liberally contributed both Money and Books. . . . It was afterwards in a Manner quite neglected, till the Year 1712, when some of the Neighbouring Clergy and Gentlemen, considering the Advantage of Parochial Libraries . . . agreed annually to contribute Twenty Shillings each to buy Books' (from the preface to *A Catalogue of Books in the Library at Wisbech*, 1718, in which 697 titles are listed). In the nineteenth century the library was moved, first to the Town Hall and then to the Museum where it is now. See F. J. Gardiner, *History of Wisbech*, 1898, pp. 87, 214–19, and for the manuscripts and the eighteenth-century Benefactors' Book, *Historical Manuscripts Commission*, 9th Report, 1883, App., pp. 293–4. Many books belonged to Thomas Turswell of King's College, Cambridge, d. 1585, for an account of whom see *Dict. Nat. Biogr.* Pepys visited the library 'where sundry very old abbey manuscripts,' 18 September 1663.

WITHAM, Essex. A 'Register of books loaned from church lending library, 1751–75, 1847–68 (2 vols.), with list of books in library, *c.* 1850'

is listed by E. J. Erith, *Essex Parish Records,* 1950, p. 234.

WITHINGTON, Herefordshire. The only evidence for the existence of a parochial library is a passage in a letter from William Brome of Withington to Thomas Hearne, 13 February 1716–17: 'Pray, do you think Plinie's Natural Hist. Lat. in usum Delp. a proper book for a Parochial Library, to be placed in the Church? We are divided here about it in our opinions, and I should be glad to know your thoughts of it': see T. Hearne, *Collections* (ed. Oxford Historical Society, 1902), vol. 6, p. 21.[1]

WOLLASTON, Northamptonshire. An S.P.C.K. library of 72 volumes was founded in 1711. Nothing of it now remains, but the original register of the books is in the Bodleian Library, MS. Top. Northants c. 42.

WOMERSLEY, Yorkshire. The incumbent records in the 'Notitia Parochialis' of 1705 (see p. 22), no. 575: 'Some Bookes of ye modern Divines as Pareus etc. lately given to ye Vicars of Womersley by Samuel Mellish of Doncaster Esqre.'

WOODBRIDGE, Suffolk [*c.* 175]. The books were bequeathed by Thomas Hewitt, rector of Bucklesham (1744–?). They were carefully catalogued in 1936 by V. B. Redstone, F.S.A. Copies of this catalogue are in the church chest and on slips in the Woodbridge Public Library. An earlier catalogue dated 1785 is in the church chest.

[1] Mr. Ian Philip kindly drew attention to this reference.

WOODCHURCH, Cheshire [45]. The books are mainly of the seventeenth and eighteenth centuries and are kept at the rectory. One of them is inscribed "July the 9th 1727 the Gift of the Revd. Mr. Thomas Green Rector of Woodchurch for an Addition to the Library there and for the perpetual use chiefly of the Ministers that shall be hereafter Resident there.' Green was rector 1705–47. 'A catalogue of the Woodchurch Library October 1819' is in the custody of the rector. A list of the books was sent to the Central Council for the Care of Churches.

WOOTTON WAWEN, Warwickshire [11]. George Dunscomb, vicar, d. 1652, 'gave some good books for the use of his Parishioners, which were preserved in the Vicaredge House, till at the request of the people they were chained to a Desk in the South Isle of the Church, April 11th, 1693': see Streeter, p. 292, quoting Thomas Baker. The photograph in Streeter, p. 291, shows the desk with 9 books chained. The books are listed in *Notes and Queries*, 5th Series, vol. 8 (1877), p. 325. See pl. IV (*c*) of this publication.

WORSBOROUGH, Yorkshire [?]. The library of the old Grammar School includes books which were given for the use of the lecturer and vicar of the church and their successors. It is now kept at the vicarage. There are catalogues of 1695, 1705 (modern copy at University College, Oxford) and 1774, when the books numbered 588. See *Notes and Queries*, vol. 12 (1855), p. 298; J. Wilkinson, *Worsborough*, 1872, pp. 378–81; P. J. Wallis in *Yorkshire Archaeological Journal*, vol. 153 (1956), p. 159.

WOTTON-UNDER-EDGE, Gloucestershire [*c.*300]. A library was bequeathed to the parish by John Okes, vicar of Whitegate, Cheshire, 1665–90, d. 1710: see S. Rudder, *History of Gloucestershire*, 1779, p. 851. According to R. Bigland, *Gloucestershire*, Supplement, pt. 9 (1889), under Wotton-under-Edge, there were 'sexcentos aut plures libros.' A typescript catalogue made in 1906 is kept in the church.

YELDEN, Bedfordshire [*c.*300]. A collection of books, some of them earlier than 1800, is in the rectory, by bequest of E. S. Bunting, rector, d. 1849: see *Notes and Queries*, 5th Series, vol. 8 (1877), p. 325.

YORK, S. Mary Castlegate. The incumbent records in the 'Notitia Parochialis' of 1705 (see p. 22), no. 1128: 'Here is a Library settling for ye Rector and his Successors being a Room in Sr Henry Thomson's Hospital late Alderman of this City and Parish wch joyns upon ye Churchyard, but tho the Room be in my Possession, yet ye Design advances slowly.'

MEDIEVAL MANUSCRIPTS NOW BELONGING TO PARISH CHURCHES OR NOW OR FORMERLY IN LIBRARIES IN-CLUDED IN THE ALPHABETICAL LIST OF PAROCHIAL LIBRARIES

APPLEBY MAGNA, Leicester-shire. Bible, thirteenth century. Given in 1702 : see J. Nichols, *History of Leicestershire,* vol. 4, pt. 2, 1811, p. 434. Now deposited at the Leicester Museum.

BATH, Somerset. The seventeenth-century catalogue lists 2 or 3 medieval manuscripts, including a Polychroni-con. They are now missing.

BEDFORD. See Alphabetical List.

BOSTON, Lincolnshire. Augustine, on Genesis, twelfth century. Formerly belonging to the Cluniac priory of Pontefract.

BRENT ELEIGH, Suffolk. See Alphabetical List.

BRIDGNORTH, Shropshire.
1. The abbreviation of Gregory's Moralia on Job attributed to Adalbertus Levita, twelfth cen-tury.
2. Statuta Angliae, *c.* 1300.

BRISTOL, All Saints.
1. William of Auvergne, Sermones de tempore, etc., fifteenth cen-tury.
2. Gerhard Zerbolt of Zutphen, de spiritualibus ascensionibus, etc., fifteenth century.

3. Augustine, de Trinitate, written in 1465 at the convent of nuns of the Third Order of S. Francis at Kempen, near Crefeld.
These 3 manuscripts have been described briefly by T. W. Williams, *Transactions of the Bristol and Glou-cestershire Archaeological Society,* vol. 31 (1908), pp. 88–9. A fourth volume noted by Williams as manuscript is in fact printed.

BRISTOL, S. Thomas the Martyr. Bible, *c.* 1400. 'Restored to ye Chirche' in 1567 : see Williams, *loc. cit.,* p. 90.

BUCKINGHAM. Bible, thir-teenth century. Given probably in 1481, but later alienated. Restored by gift in 1883.

BURY ST. EDMUNDS, Suffolk.
1. (a) Bede, Historia Ecclesiastica, etc., *c.* 1400.
   (b) Bede, Commentaries on Acts and Catholic Epistles, thir-teenth century.
   Formerly belonging to the abbey of Syon, Middlesex. Given in 1595.
2. Cassian, Collationes, fifteenth century. Belonged to the Domus Clericorum of Doesborch in Holland.

3. Pauline Epistles, glossed, late twelfth century. Given in 1639.
4. Medical texts, etc., twelfth and thirteenth centuries, partly in Beneventan script. From the abbey of Bury.

Nos. 3 and 4 are described by M. R. James, *On the Abbey of S. Edmund at Bury,* Cambridge Antiquarian Society, Octavo Series, no. 28 (1895), pp. 50, 53, 67.

COLCHESTER, S. Mary, Essex. Bible, thirteenth century. Belonged to a fifteenth-century rector, William Kettell. Bought for the church at Sotheby's, 29 November 1949, lot 1.

EASTBOURNE, S. Mary, Sussex. Book of Hours given in or before 1929 by Miss Davies-Gilbert: see *Sussex Notes and Queries,* vol. 2 (1929), p. 61.

HODNET, Shropshire. Book of Hours, fifteenth century.

HULL, Holy Trinity, Yorkshire. For a now missing Bible, see Alphabetical List.

IPSWICH, Suffolk. See Alphabetical List.

LANGLEY MARISH, Buckinghamshire.
1. The 'Kederminster Gospels,' written in England in the first half of the eleventh century. Belonged formerly to the college of Windsor. At present on deposit at the British Museum.
2. Petrus Riga, Aurora, early thirteenth century. At present on deposit with the Bucks Archaeological Society, Aylesbury.

LEICESTER. The Leicester Codex of the New Testament in Greek was given to the Town Library in 1645. It is not known whether the 5 other medieval manuscripts, a Bible, a volume of the sermons attributed to Wyclif in English, a volume of miscellaneous tracts and two copies of the Statutes belonged to the library before it was moved from S. Martin's in 1632. For them, see *Historical Manuscripts Commission,* 8th Report (1881), Appendix, pp. 419–25.

LONDON, S. Martin-in-the-Fields. See Alphabetical List.

LONDON, S. Peter Cornhill. Bible, late thirteenth century. Given to a chantry chapel in the church in the Middle Ages, but later alienated. Recovered by purchase in the nineteenth century. They are now kept at the Guildhall. See R. A. Rye, *Guide to the Libraries of London,* 3rd ed. 1927, p. 16.

MAIDSTONE, Kent.
1. The second volume of the 'Lambeth Bible,' twelfth century. See E. G. Millar in *Bulletin de la Société Française de Reproductions de Manuscrits à Peintures,* vol. 8 (1924), pp. 17–18, 29–31.
2. Sermons and notes for preachers, including brief texts in French and English, thirteenth century. Belonged, *c.* 1300, to a member of the Hospital of S. John the Baptist at Northampton. See

C. Brown in *Modern Language Review,* vol. 21 (1926), pp. 1–12, 249–60.
3. A Book of Hours and Psalter, fifteenth century.

These manuscripts are now deposited with the rest of the All Saints' Library at the Maidstone Museum.

MALMESBURY, Wiltshire.
1. Bible in 4 volumes written in the fifteenth century by a Flemish scribe, Gerard Brilis, for the Charterhouse of La Chapelle at Hérinnes lez Enghien, near Brussels. Belonged to Mrs. Audley Lovell of Cole Park, Malmesbury. Sold at Sotheby's, 19 June 1914, lot 138. Given to the church in the same year by Lord Suffolk.
2. Genesis, Ruth and Psalms in French, *c.* 1400. Signatures of members of the Stumpe and Baynton families, sixteenth-century, connect the manuscript with Malmesbury. Given by James P. R. Lyell, d. 1949.

MINEHEAD, Somerset. Missal, fifteenth century. Formerly the property of Richard Fitzjames, rector 1485, bishop of London 1506–22. Bought for the church at Sotheby's, 29 November 1949, lot 13.

NEWCASTLE - UPON - TYNE, Northumberland.
1. Bible, thirteenth century. Formerly belonging to the Augustinian priory of Hexham, Northumberland.
2. Richard Rolle, Commentary on Psalms and Canticles in English,

late fourteenth century. Given in 1660. Now deposited at the Central Public Library, after having been found at S. Nicholas's (now the Cathedral) by J. T. Fowler, 'tumbling about in a drawer among old magazines and Newcastle dust.' See *Notes and Queries,* 5th Series, vol. 1 (1874), p. 41.

NORWICH, S. Andrew. See Alphabetical List.

NORWICH, S. Peter Mancroft, Norfolk.
1. Pauline Epistles, glossed, early thirteenth century.
2. Bible, thirteenth century.

OAKHAM, Rutland. Bible, thirteenth century. Given in 1599.

RANWORTH, Norfolk. Antiphonal, fifteenth century. Almost certainly at Ranworth in medieval times. Bought in 1912 from Messrs. Ellis (cat. 140, item 1, with facsimile), who obtained it in the Huth sale, Sotheby's, 15 November 1911, lot 217 (facsimile). See W. H. Frere's introduction to *Antiphonale Sarisburiense,* Plainsong and Medieval Music Society, vol. 1 (1901–15), p. 79.

REIGATE, Surrey.
1. Bernard Gui, Catalogus Romanorum Pontificum, etc., later fourteenth century. Given in 1701.
2. Bible, thirteenth century. In a Cambridge University loan chest in 1453. Given in 1705.
3. Books of Hours, fifteenth cen-

tury. Formerly belonging to Franciscan nuns of Aldgate, London. Given in 1701.

4. Meditations of S. Bonaventura and others, fifteenth century. Given in 1701.

ROMSEY, Hampshire. Psalter, fifteenth century. Bought *c.* 1900. See H. G. D. Liveing, *Records of Romsey Abbey*, 1906, pp. 285–302. The Psalter appears to have belonged to a member of the Benedictine nunnery at Winchester.

SHIPDHAM, Norfolk. See Alphabetical List.

STEEPLE ASHTON, Wiltshire. Book of Hours, fifteenth century. See Alphabetical List.

SWAFFHAM, Norfolk. Sarum Book of Hours, fifteenth century.

TIVERTON, Devon. Book of Hours, fifteenth century. See Alphabetical List.

WHITCHURCH, Hampshire. See Alphabetical List.

WIMBORNE, Dorset. Regimen Animarum, fourteenth century.

WISBECH, Cambridgeshire. 8 of the 9 manuscripts are noticed by M. R. James, *On the Abbey of S. Edmund at Bury,* Cambridge Antiquarian Society, Octavo Series, no. 28 (1895), pp. 46, 71, 86–7, and by N. R. Ker, *Medieval Libraries of Great Britain,* 1941, p. 14. The 9th manuscript is a copy of Wyclif's sermons in English.

WOLLATON, Nottinghamshire. Antiphonal, fifteenth century. Given in or shortly after 1460, but later alienated. Restored by gift of Lord Middleton in 1925.

ADDENDA

BROUGHTON. Except for 18 books and a dozen pamphlets which are being retained at the church, the whole collection was sold to Cambridge University Library in 1958. About half of it, comprising all the books which were duplicates of books in the University Library, was then resold to a bookseller. The sale to Cambridge University was under faculty granted by the Consistory Court of the Diocese of Ely. Lists of the books and pamphlets sold by Cambridge University Library and of the books and pamphlets retained at Broughton were made for the Central Council for the Care of Churches.

BUCKLAND, Berkshire [17]. The books, mainly seventeenth-century and in Latin, were transferred in 1951 to the Old Manor House, Buckland, for safe-keeping.

ELHAM. A catalogue was printed in 1845: *A Catalogue of Mr. Lee Warly's Library bequeathed by him to the Parish of Elham in 1809: restored by public subscription in 1843.* London (W. Congreve) 1845.

LAWSHALL. It is planned to transfer this library to the Moyses Hall, Bury St. Edmunds.

LONDON, S. Leonard, Shoreditch. The books in this library have recently been re-bound in red morocco.

OXFORD, S. Peter-le-Bailey. A roll of parchment containing a list of 'The Books in S^t· Peters Church' in 1731 is now in the possession of S. Peter's Hall, Oxford. 31 books, all in English, are listed, together with 'one box with Two Shelves in it for to put ye Books in it with a Lock and Key to ye s^d Box.' Ten of the books are the same as those provided by the S.P.C.K. for their libraries (Burnet, Goodman, Nelson, Ostervald (2), Scott (5): see pp. 35–7).

SKIPTON. There is a good description of the library by John A. Woods, 'The Petyt Library, Skipton.' *Books: National Book League Journal,* no. 289, November 1954.

SLAPTON. A catalogue of the library made in 1727 and papers concerning it are in a manuscript belonging to the Episcopal Registry at Salisbury (*Historical Manuscripts Commission, Various Collections,* vol. 4 (1907), p. 22).

TORTWORTH. About 200 seventeenth-century and eighteenth-century books labelled 'Tortworth Rectory' and containing usually the book-plate of John Bosworth (rector, d. 1786) are in the library of Oriel College, Oxford. These books came to Oriel in 1921: see *Oriel College Record,* vol. 4, pt. 2 (1922), p. 105.

The lists of books mentioned in the text as having been sent to or made for the Central Council for the Care of Churches (e.g. pp. 66, 68) have been given to the Bodleian Library by the Central Council.

TABLE OF PAROCHIAL LIBRARIES FOUNDED BEFORE 1800 AND STILL EXISTING IN 1959, BY COUNTIES[1]

* indicates that the library has been moved from its original home. To find its present home, the list on pp. 28–9 should be consulted.

** indicates that part of the library has been moved.

*/ indicates that less than 10 books survive.

ENGLAND

BEDFORDSHIRE
*Bedford
Bromham

BERKSHIRE
Denchworth
Sutton Courtenay

BUCKINGHAMSHIRE
Langley Marish
*Mentmore

CAMBRIDGESHIRE
Bassingbourne
*Graveley
*Wisbech

CHESHIRE
Halton
Nantwich
Woodchurch

CORNWALL
Lanteglos-by-Camelford
*/Lostwithiel
Newquay

CUMBERLAND
*/Ainstable
*/Dalston

DERBYSHIRE
*Norton

DEVON
*Barnstaple
Crediton
Kingsbridge
Ottery St. Mary
Plymtree
Tiverton
Totnes

DORSET
Gillingham
*/Milton Abbas
Wimborne

COUNTY DURHAM
Darlington

ESSEX
Chelmsford
Hatfield Broad Oak
Maldon
Newport

GLOUCESTERSHIRE
Bristol, All Saints
*Stonehouse
Tortworth
Wotton-under-Edge

HAMPSHIRE
Basingstoke
*/Whitchurch

[1] See pp. 46–7 for eight existing libraries founded after 1800 and included in the alphabetical list on pp. 64–107.

P

HEREFORDSHIRE
Hereford, All Saints

HERTFORDSHIRE
*Bushey

HUNTINGDONSHIRE
**Broughton
Offord Cluny
St. Neots

KENT
*Ash-by-Wrotham
*Crundale
Doddington
*Maidstone
Preston-by-Wingham

LANCASHIRE
Astley
*Bolton-le-Moors
Cartmel
Flookburgh
Gorton
Poulton-le-Fylde
*/Ribchester
*Salford, Sacred Trinity
Turton

LEICESTERSHIRE
Ashby-de-la-Zouch
*Cole Orton
**Loughborough

LINCOLNSHIRE
Boston
**Grantham
Sleaford
*Spalding
Stamford

LONDON
*London, S. Leonard, Shoreditch

MIDDLESEX
*/Hillingdon

NORFOLK
*Great Yarmouth

*King's Lynn
*/Norwich, S. Peter Mancroft
*Shipdham
Swaffham

NORTHAMPTONSHIRE
Finedon
King's Cliffe

NORTHUMBERLAND
*Alnwick
**Newcastle-upon-Tyne

NOTTINGHAMSHIRE
*Elston
Newark-on-Trent

OXFORDSHIRE
Bloxham
*Henley-on-Thames

RUTLAND
Oakham

SHROPSHIRE
Bridgnorth
Chirbury
Dudleston
More
Tong
Wentnor
Whitchurch

SOMERSET
*Bath
*Martock

SUFFOLK
Assington
Beccles
Bury St. Edmunds
Coddenham
Lawshall
Nayland
Stoke-by-Nayland
Woodbridge

SURREY
*/Effingham
Reigate

114

SUSSEX
*/Amberley
Heathfield

WARWICKSHIRE
*Birmingham, S. Martin
*Birmingham, S. Philip
*King's Norton
Sheldon
**Warwick, S. Mary
Wootton Wawen

WESTMORLAND
Bampton
Beetham

WILTSHIRE
*Marlborough

WORCESTERSHIRE
Bromsgrove
Feckenham
*/Norton-cum-Lenchwick

YORKSHIRE
Beverley

Bradfield
Bridlington
*/*Bubwith
East Harlsey
*/Ecclesfield
Hackness
Halifax
*Hull, Holy Trinity
Hull, S. Mary Lowgate
Kildwick
*Skipton
Slaithwaite
Stainton
*Tankersley
Worsborough

WALES AND MONMOUTHSHIRE

MONMOUTHSHIRE
*Caerleon
*Newport

MONTGOMERYSHIRE
Darowen

INDEX

[1] The entries under the sub-headings 'belonging to,' 'for use of,' and 'given to,' provide a rough guide to information given in the text. It should be remembered that not all the evidence there adduced concerning the use and ownership of libraries is authoritative

The Parochial Libraries of the Church of England *is set in 12 point Baskerville type, one point leaded. The compositor was E. Salmon, the pressman F. Mabbutt and the binder A. Heasman, all of the Faith Press. The edition is limited to 500 copies of which this is number* 313